THE GAME OF VALUE CREATION

Think, Make Decisions, and Create
Value Like an Active Shareholder

KARL YAACOUB

MINDSTIR MEDIA

Published by Mindstir Media, LLC
45 Lafayette Rd | Suite 181| North Hampton, NH 03862 | USA
1.800.767.0531 | www.mindstirmedia.com

Printed in the United States of America

ISBN: 979-8-9860614-7-4

Everyone must leave something behind when he dies, my grandfather said. A child or a book or a painting or a house or a wall built or a pair of shoes made. Or a garden planted. Something your hand touched some way so your soul has somewhere to go when you die, and when people look at that tree or that flower you planted, you're there. . . The difference between the man who just cuts lawns and a real gardener is in the touching, he said. The lawn-cutter might just as well not have been there at all; the gardener will be there a lifetime.

—Ray Bradbury, Fahrenheit 451

DEDICATION

To my wife, Hannah, and my brother, Ralph. Without
your encouragement and support, I wouldn't have
been able to write this book. I am grateful.

TABLE OF CONTENTS

Foreword xi

Introduction 1
   All About Legacy 2
   The Big Picture 4
   Sculpting with Acumen 6
   Limitless 7
      Enabling Value Creation 9
   Expecting the Expected 13

Legacy-Governance Synergy 17
   The Board of Directors 20
      Common Types of Committees 23
   Deconstructing Structure 26
      Organizational Structure Best Practices 29
      Key Considerations 30
   An Invisible Dream Team: Policies, Procedures, Processes, and Systems 31
   The Risk Canceling Equation 33
      Relevant Questions 35
   Reporting as a Source of Power 36
   Who Is Your Auditor? 37
   Companies Outlive Great Leaders 39

The Business Continuity Perspective 41
    TAKE ACTION: Governance Boosting Exercise 42

Numbers Game 45
  Become Intimate with Your Financial Statements 46
  Have Your Key Figures Handy 52
    Mastering Financial Housekeeping 53
    Unlock Trapped Cash 56
    Avoid The Cost-Cutting Obsession 57
  Funding Outside the Box 59
    The Dual Power of Debt 61
    Alternative Financing 62
  Know Your Worth 65
  Common Valuation Methodologies 66
  Additional Valuation Considerations 70
  From Private to Public via IPO 71
    Pros and Cons of Going Public 72
  Closing Remarks on The Numerical Hocus Pocus 73
    TAKE ACTION: Cash Boosting Exercise 75

Bulletproof Strategy 77
  Taming the Market Forces 79
  Market Forces 80
    All About Benchmarking 84
    Competition Analysis Checklist 84
  Budgeting and Planning in the Age of Disruption 86
    Budget vs. Business Plan 86
    To Sell or Not to Sell 90
    TAKE ACTION: Develop Effective Marketing
    and Sales Strategies 90
  Building and Pricing for Profit 92
    Product Strategy Considerations 93
    The Almighty Dollar 94
    TAKE ACTION: Pricing for Profit 95
  Smooth Operations 96
    TAKE ACTION: Steps to Boost Operational Efficiencies ... 98

The Subtle Art of Company Culture......................................99
TAKE ACTION: Suggested Steps to Improve
Company Culture 101
Leveraging Technology in the Space Age 101
Dominate Intangible Assets 104
TAKE ACTION: Maximize and Monetize
Intangible Asset Value 106
Scaling Just Right 107
TAKE ACTION: Suggested Steps to Scalability.............109
Inorganic Strategy 110
Checklist: Exploring Growth Through M&A.................113
The Buyer Questionnaire 114
Selling Moves 116
Business Seller – Opportunity Overview Template 117
Keeping Promises 122
M&A Jargon Is Just Jargon..132
Concluding Organic and Inorganic Corporate Strategy ...136
Next Steps: Corporate Strategies You Can Start
Adopting Today...137

Magical Charisma..139
Looking at The Stars 140
Passing the Torch...147
Rationalizing the Irrational..148
We are Irrational Beings 149
Limiting Beliefs..151
Leveraging Weaknesses 152
Demystifying CHANGE...153
Efficient Change Management 154
Last Mile 156
TAKE ACTION: Get the Ball Rolling Today................157

What Dreams May Come 159
Enabling The Enablers 159
Value Creation Enablers 160
Wisdom Bites...160

Sharpening Your Sword 163
    The Power of Kaizen 165
Moving Forward and Next Steps 166
    Final Case Study..166

Closing Remarks.. 171

References 173

About The Author 177

FOREWORD

There's much to consider when running a business in making your venture a success. Today's business needs people who understand the mission. As an entrepreneur, I know that there are several important steps that business managers can take to ensure that their venture is successful now, and in the years to come. Mindstir Media began small but is growing by leaps and bounds while utilizing the strategies laid out in Karl Yaacoub's book "The Game of Value Creation". He shares the insider knowledge invaluable to those wanting to make the most of their business and breaks down solid business rules and strategies that can be utilized by professionals in any industry.

With more than 11 years of experience creating shareholder value combined with engineering education, Mr. Yaacoub was not only highly qualified to deliver a compelling message, but he also demonstrated the drive to author a publication to share his experience and knowledge with the reader. His engineering background brands him as a problem solver, and his international network of peers brands him as a global player. Combine this with his international financial experience, and he is even more qualified to tie his message to the financial goals of investors and corporations. As someone with experience in private equity and investment banking, Karl Yaacoub has extensive experience helping businesses surpass stakeholder expectations, achieve sustainable financial goals, and succeed in implementing desired strategies.

"The Game of Value Creation" uses a deep understanding of owner expectations, and sustainable financial goals tied to smart business practices, for success. This "no-nonsense" approach to corporate value creation focuses on proven business methodology and tactics to enhance and prolong the life of any operating business. Karl Yaacoub's personal experience with what bankers and investors look at when considering investing money in businesses gives him a unique perspective that can point business managers in the right direction to maximize their businesses.

Readers can expect to attain new strategies that will be invaluable to their business, no matter the type. Learn the secrets to building a legacy from an institutional investment insider, and see your visions become reality!

J.J. Hebert, USA Today bestselling author

INTRODUCTION

*The things you do for yourself are gone when you are gone,
but the things you do for others remain as your legacy.*

—Kalu Ndukwe Kalu

A legacy is more than just a tally of our memories from the past; it's the root that allows us to grow in the present and see into the future. Young trees grow better in soil that contains remnants of older trees, and the same goes for humans. In order to thrive and prosper, we need the foundation of achievements, the rhizome of experiences, and the lessons of the past.

A legacy is sometimes thought of as being something that just happens to us without our active participation. However, what if we were to place our legacy, or that of our company, at the center of every step we make on our journey?

Wouldn't it be more meaningful to form an interconnection across the decades, to feel a sense of deep connection to the past and the future, to build something that will withstand the test of time and be revered by future generations?

ALL ABOUT LEGACY

Legacy is a fundamental part of what it is to be human. When people think about leaving a legacy, they can add a whole lot of meaning to their lives. By exploring the concept of legacy, we gain insight into human relationships and thriving communities, as well as the hidden depths of the human spirit.

In spite of its association with death in popular culture, legacy is actually about life, not death. Although death puts our lives into perspective, how we will be remembered depends on what we do while we are alive.

Focusing on our legacy helps us choose what kind of life we want to live, what we want to learn, and how we want to inspire those who will follow us.

It can be quite emotional to contemplate our legacy. There is a wide range of emotions that can be experienced, including fear, frustration, disappointment, hope, and anxiety.

Do I have any lessons to share?

Is there anything left to aim for?

Have I fully realized my potential?

How have my actions and ideas benefited my community and others?

And the biggest question of all, how will I be remembered?

We don't have to win the Nobel Prize to be proud of our legacy; this elusive testimony of our existence can take many forms.

Leaving a legacy can mean having a loving family, running a successful business, writing a memorable book, building a community, or preserving wisdom. Perhaps you simply made a lasting impact on others through kind words or actions, without realizing it at the time.

Are you living your life in a way that will allow your values, dreams, talents, and beliefs to reflect your legacy?

It is human to worry about your legacy, to have a sense that your life has some meaning in the vastness of the human experience. Edmund Burke once wrote that society involves "a partnership not only between those who are living, but between those who are living, those who are dead, and those who are to be born." As we go through life, making decisions about our businesses, careers, and personal lives, we must consider this partnership. It is this special connection to our ancestors and future generations that makes us unique as a species. Legacy is about contributing to that chain of communication and passing on the lessons of the past to build a better future.

In business, a legacy isn't just about the products and services a company provides; it's about the connections it has built with generations of stakeholders. Trust, nostalgia, and tradition drive the buying decision of a person who purchases a truck from a brand they have used for generations in their family. When a person buys an engagement ring from a store on Fifth Avenue in New York because it has always been where "the family buys jewelry", they are buying into something more than just a ring. Aside from nostalgia, they are buying trust, warmth, and special treatment. When investors pass on their stock holdings in the company they built or invested in, to their kids and grandchildren, their legacy also lives on.

The legacy of a business connects stakeholders and founders with future generations. Their happy customers become brand ambassadors; the people and the institutions they have built long-term relationships with, will continue to offer business opportunities in the long run. Employees who believe they were, or are, part of that legacy perform better and contribute more to the company's success. By making use of the legacy, stakeholders can continue to give back to society, leaving everyone better off. Even after the founders and owners leave, everything they have built will continue to live on and be cherished.

THE BIG PICTURE

Dreams are never pursued with the expectation of mediocre results. It's not to fail and learn a lesson that we get into business and partnerships. It's because we want to get closer to our dreams. When it comes to our endeavors, we are not just in it for the experience; we also want to succeed and reap the rewards. For all that we have built and contributed, we hope to be recognized and appreciated.

This book will help you realize that there is more to your business journey, even if you're well on your way to being totally hands-off. Your legacy extends far beyond what you have done. In addition, you will have a framework that you can use to manifest "what could have been".

As a result, you will likely start asking better questions and your discussions will become more engaging. As soon as you begin implementing the low-hanging fruit presented here, you will end up in a better position than when you began, and you will see results as early as the first few months.

There will be an upbeat tone when talking about your business, what it stands for, and what it represents. Business progress will become clearer not only to you, but to those you matter to in your sphere, the stakeholders, and the decision-makers.

Instead of obsessing over maintaining control and micromanagement, you are going to obsess over creating value, improving your customers' buying journey, innovating, unlocking more cash to fund growth projects, and developing other leaders.

You will be able to better understand how the market changes, how your organization should adapt, and how your target customers think. Your trust in growth will grow, and you will ensure those in your sphere of influence are also on the same journey, because they have chosen to be.

Value creation frameworks used by private equity firms, Fortune 500 companies, and top blue-chip companies around the world have a lot in common with the framework outlined in this book. The main pillars of these frameworks are corporate governance, strategic finance, organic and inorganic strategy, and exemplary leadership.

When you strive for excellence across these key pillars, you will discover what remains of your hidden value.

SCULPTING WITH ACUMEN

Business interruption is not a concern for those whose processes and systems run smoothly when they are away. They can step away from day-to-day operations without being compulsively worried about things breaking down. The company's operations are run so efficiently that they can fully focus their attention on something more valuable, or even something entirely unrelated.

With the systems they've put in place, they don't need to be physically present for every small decision or cost item to be approved, as well as every single deliverable to be monitored.

In their organization, the right people are in the right places and they follow the right processes and systems. They know that their team is capable and reliable, so it doesn't make sense to micromanage or tell them what to do. Instead, they grant them autonomy, support them, and trust that the job will get done because it always does.

Those who build legacy businesses do not resist change or insist on doing things the same way they always have. Innovating and trying something new does not frighten them, and they are not afraid to shake the tree a little to see what happens. As a result, they are able to come to a decision based on their assessment of the bigger picture. They do not obsessively dwell on their ideas, and therefore, are able to take calculated risks without becoming paralyzed by change.

With their executive presence, they inspire others to be like them. Rather than draining others of their energy, they replenish it. They know that results speak louder than words, and that being overworked or busy is not necessarily a sign of success.

They are aware that if they have the right people in the right places, using the right tools and doing the right things, they will consistently get the right results.

Rather than wasting their finite energy on small tasks, they realize it is significantly more efficient to use their finite energy on big ideas. Ultimately, they want to make sure their business is successful in the long run. Even without them, the business will continue to thrive.

LIMITLESS

Due to the era of giant shifts, gone are the days when a lack of resources was the main hindrance to business growth. By today's standards, what used to be considered a lean machine is no longer considered agile, and many industries have changed the way they do business.

Obtaining data is easier than ever, and there is no shortage of technology capable of crunching millions of data points and coming up with findings, insights, and trends. There is so much information available that the limiting factor lies more in how you use it and how resistant humans are to embracing change and adopting technology.

You don't need complex or expensive tools to provide employees with access to information they need. It is no longer necessary to spend millions of dollars on infrastructure to reduce costs or automate functions like payroll. Fewer tools that are well-integrated result in fewer mistakes, greater transparency, and better collaboration between departments.

Skills that were once highly valued are becoming increasingly commoditized and replaced by lower-cost labor and technology.

As a result, customers have become more demanding of corporations. And increasingly, they are more willing to pay a premium for convenience, consistency, and an improved buying experience.

Businesses should strive to be the best corporations that they can be in order to continue to remain competitive and relevant in their markets. There will be a detailed discussion of what that entails within this book, but here is a brief overview:

- A decentralized decision-making setup with low key-man risk
- A consistent delivery of high-quality products and a positive customer experience
- A framework for minimizing human error and taking calculated risks
- A framework for ensuring profitable, sustainable, and seamless operations
- Allocation of company resources toward reinvestment and growth
- A continuous exploration of alliances, joint ventures, acquisitions, and new markets
- A systematic approach to the development of intangible assets (e.g. branding)

There is an encouraging thought here in that every business has components and strengths that are unique to its setup. One example is a popular product that has consistently maintained its quality. Another example is the expertise of the management team and the combined experience of the employees. Also, the brand that people have grown to love, and the relationships with key stakeholders. These are all unique assets to a company.

Therefore, it is important to realize that no matter how big or small a company is, it will never start its value creation journey from zero. In reality, there are many desirable characteristics that can be built upon, which implies that there is an abundance of value and potential waiting to be realized by employing the right strategies.

The fact that we have become accustomed to doing things a certain way that has worked for us in the past can easily make us overlook this potential. In particular, if we have a lot on our plate at once, we tend to prioritize the task at hand and ignore transformational solutions that may seem too expensive or impossible to implement at the moment.

If we take a step back for a moment, what will we see? Instead of focusing on what is already there, what if we began creating value deliberately?

Enabling Value Creation

Taking part in a journey of transformational change requires us to acknowledge our limitations, weaknesses, and strengths, as well as operate within the parameters of our stress and irritability thresholds.

It is essential that we face down problems as they are and point them out for what they are: problems.

In order to do so successfully, we need to be asking the right questions. In some cases, it will be necessary to dig a little deeper in order to come up with these questions, and that's perfectly fine. However, it is important that no stone is left unturned in this process, since the better questions we ask, the more relevant and achievable our proposed solutions will become.

As long as we focus on things we can control, manage risk, and maintain positive relationships with those around us, we'll be just fine. We will be more prepared to face change and uncertainty in the future.

If you observe business leaders who consistently and effectively get things done, you will notice that they often tend to operate with a sense of conviction and purpose. These leaders know that the best time to take action is now. By putting reason and empirical observations before their beliefs, they make sound decisions. And although they recognize they are taking risks, those risks are calculated and even asymmetric at times, meaning they are more likely than not to produce favorable outcomes.

Let's put on our thinking caps and begin our journey together.

In order to create greater corporate value and leave a lasting legacy, the following enablers are essential:

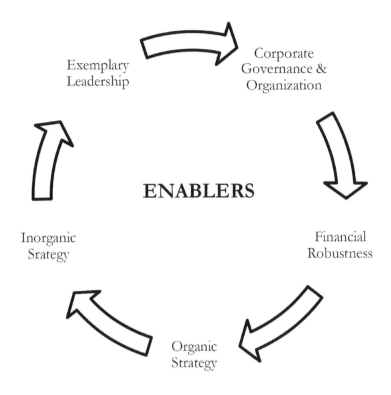

By the end of the governance section in this book, you should have a clear understanding of how you can set up an effective governance infrastructure within a company. A wide range of ideas will be offered for designing an effective organizational structure and establishing and implementing the right processes, policies, procedures, and systems. An emphasis will be placed on decision-making processes and operational transparency. As you progress through the first enabler, you will also learn how to identify and reduce risk, facilitate a sound auditing process, and organize internal reporting.

In the next section, titled Numbers Game, we will demystify financials so you can understand key numerical data and financial documents regardless of your background. Budgeting, releasing trapped cash, and allocating funds where they will bring the most benefit will all be covered. If you are having difficulty obtaining funding for projects, this chapter will highlight key considerations for several types of funding in detail. This section also discusses various methods of valuing businesses and why you might want to go public.

We will examine two types of strategy in the following chapter, titled "Bulletproof Strategy"; organic strategy which leverages existing resources and capabilities, and inorganic strategy which focuses on acquiring companies through mergers and acquisitions (M&A). By highlighting key components to focus on within any business, we propose tactics that can help businesses maximize growth and achieve better efficiencies. From product strategy to pricing, leveraging technology, maximizing intangible assets, and growing inorganically through M&A, this section will cover a wide range of strategic ideas and initiatives that will be sure to push your business forward.

For our last enabler, we will discuss the soft skills and behavioral attributes needed to make the journey of transformational change more enjoyable for everyone involved. A number of topics are discussed, including the traits with which successful corporate leaders are characterized, maximizing executive presence, identifying and developing new leaders, and managing change. The impact of cognitive biases on behavior is also discussed in detail to help you limit their influence.

You will find in each chapter a list of questions or action steps so that you can begin making an impact right away. These chapters are brief, straightforward, and action-oriented. You will not find long tales about business management in this book, but a plethora of methods and techniques used by some of the most successful companies in the world that can be applied in varying degrees to any business setting.

While there is no magic wand that will solve all your business problems tomorrow, I am almost certain that this book will provide you with exciting insights. The series of relevant questions suggested here will help you think about value creation differently. You will also be presented with new solutions, so things will look a little brighter for your business.

There is more to this book than business success; it is about creating something that will endure, and obtaining the best position you possibly can in business. Using the strategies and tactics described here, companies can remain competitive long after those who founded them, or who currently lead them, have retired. That is the true meaning of corporate legacy.

EXPECTING THE EXPECTED

Perhaps you might be a little skeptical about me and would like to know if I am qualified to write about value creation and corporate legacy. Please continue reading the next couple of pages if that is the case.

After years of accumulating knowledge and experience in the fields of international banking and active investing, I have decided to distill a practical application of the lessons learned, and to help others by sharing my perspective, thoughts, and convictions.

Having worked at both a global bank and a public investment firm, I was given the opportunity to source investment opportunities, value businesses, negotiate, execute, and close deals, as well as help put portfolio companies on the same path outlined here.

The goal was to make these companies richer, more sustainable, and more impactful. In most cases, the transaction size would range between USD 50 million and USD 300 million, and depending on our appetite, financial capabilities, and size of the deal, we would either acquire a minority shareholding or a majority shareholding in prospective target companies.

The purpose of my work is to provide you with significant value, and to genuinely help you, because that is the only way I can derive a sense of meaning from it myself. Here are some things to expect:

- An overarching, 360-degree framework for corporate growth, sustainability, and maximum impact.

- Actionable steps, not simply information, to help you focus on the big picture and the most important things.

- Well-thought-out questions that will lead to better solutions through root cause analysis.

Upon completing the last page of this book, you will be able to leverage a proven, effective, and employable framework for value creation that applies to corporate governance, organic and inorganic strategy, and strategic finance.

If you've ever wondered how companies do what they do, this book is for you.

It's for every business owner interested in making a bigger impact. It's for anyone interested in business or with ambition and grand ideas.

If executed correctly, the principles here could yield substantial value, since the proposed strategies are not entirely dependent on the limited resources you have at your disposal today.

This book is intended to be of use to a variety of people, ranging from small business owners to non-executive directors at multinational conglomerates.

You have come to the right place if you want to learn how to transform an ordinary business into a 2.0 business.

LEGACY-GOVERNANCE SYNERGY

*The real mechanism for corporate governance
is the active involvement of the owners.*

—Louis V. Gerstner, Jr.

What would it look like if you governed a country like you govern your own company?

Would it be a transparent and orderly nation with the right checks and controls in place? Would it safeguard the interests and wellbeing of its citizens and its ecosystem?

Or would it be chaotic and disorganized? One that is prone to falling into the abyss as soon as risks and challenges crop up?

Perhaps somewhere in the middle?

The concept of corporate governance is as old as time. It is the set of laws and processes designed to regulate and protect a business. Ultimately, it is about distributing rights and responsibilities within an organization in a way that aligns with what society and the market expect.

A good corporate governance model makes it possible for each stake-holder to identify right from wrong. Rarely will there be prolonged confusion, or any room for intentional misinterpretation. As a result, fairness, transparency, and integrity will blossom in a corporate setting.

A lack of proper corporate governance, however, leads to an "if everyone else does it, I better not question it" mentality.

An organization's corporate governance enables it to build trust with its investors and the public by assuring them that the company will be managed correctly, without any ill-intent or suspicion-inducing behavior. It enables a company to better serve the market and function as a micro-ecosystem within a macro-ecosystem.

Small and mid-sized businesses may think corporate governance is not relevant to them. I once met with an active venture capitalist who sits on a fund's investment committee. Venture capital investors generally invest in early-stage ventures. Such businesses are risky, and their success depends on the success of the founding team, whose needs and responsibilities constantly change. There is a lot that goes into founding and maintaining a successful startup, from testing, adding, and adjusting products and services to entirely changing a company's business model.

His argument was that governance is not a necessity for early-stage tech companies but would be more relevant for more established companies. We politely disagreed on the subject. Even though a company might not need a board of directors or a succession plan when it is a year old, it should still incorporate elements of decision making, controls, and transparency to get the business infrastructure ready and positioned for the rapid growth it expects. Core functions must still be defined by their responsibilities, authority limits, and scope of work as the business and its requirements evolve.

In other words, whatever stage a company is in its growth cycle, a framework for decision-making and responsibility distribution across the organization is essential for growth, efficiency, sustainability, and resilience. It is also essential to have internal controls, a risk management framework, as well as policies, procedures, processes, and systems.

There is a reason why companies with internal controls, sound policies, and efficient systems outperform their competitors. Publicly listed companies are also required by regulators to maintain high standards of governance. This will ensure that all stakeholders are protected regardless of their relationship with the company.

Does it seem irrational that a private business would be better off if it were governed like a public business?

In this chapter, we are going to discuss the inner workings of corporate governance, highlighting the benefits of adopting a robust governance framework.

Before beginning with the duties of the board of directors, let us consider the following preliminary questions:

- How likely is it that your business would thrive without you?
- Have you ever thought about creating a board of directors to oversee management in your corporation?
- How would you rate the quality of your policies, procedures, processes, and systems?

- How do authorities and responsibilities appear to be divided across the organization? In what manner do decisions appear to be made?

- Are you using a risk management framework that actively defines and monitors risks?

- How would your employees describe the way your company is run?

THE BOARD OF DIRECTORS

It is always necessary for companies to meet certain regulatory and statutory requirements, based on their type, ownership structure, and market in which they operate.

As an example, publicly listed companies on the New York Stock Exchange (NYSE) need to have a board of directors (BOD), of which the majority is comprised of independent directors. This means they should not have any direct or indirect material relationship with the company.

The key function of governance is to protect a business and the interests of all its stakeholders. And there is a lot to learn about best governance practices by simply observing how the biggest public companies in the world are governed.

Private companies can only benefit from governing themselves like publicly listed entities if they are willing to make that decision. This will help cultivate the right culture and habits as they evolve.

Although specific requirements will vary depending on the maturity cycle and the needs of a business, as part of its main duties, a board of directors

(BOD) might need to make decisions regarding recommendations and requests from management, evaluate management performance, and protect minority shareholders' interests.

As a governing board, the BOD usually leaves day-to-day responsibilities to the executive leadership team; however, it retains the final decision over matters such as hiring the management team, entering new markets, approving acquisitions, and paying dividends to shareholders.

If the board feels it needs to be a hand-holder to get management on track, that may be a red flag. If the board is only approving or rejecting items without adding value to the most pressing and important decisions that drive a corporation, that would also be a red flag.

If the members of the BOD lack the appropriate skills or are simply not engaged enough, it is likely that the board meetings will be treated as formalities. A board's members need to be proficient and skilled in the topic they are reviewing and opining on to add meaningful value. It is imperative that they understand the industry, the business ecosystem, and the specifics of the business they are governing.[i] They need to be intimately aware of what is going on with the entity they govern, so they can formulate their independent thinking, and not just rely on what the management team puts in front of them.

Perhaps the board is seeing external threats in the market that the management team needs to address, such as industry disruptions from technology startups or a larger competitor entering the market. The management team can present a mitigating strategy to the board incorporating such concerns if such threats are communicated. By doing so, the board will be able to provide feedback on such strategies and add value in areas within its expertise and capabilities.

Consequently, everyone involved becomes more aware of expectations, and board duties would no longer be dominated by the practice of checking boxes.

It is important to have the most qualified people on the board of directors, given the duty of care to shareholders and the level of responsibility the board has. An effective board does more than add significant value to a company; it protects the business's interests and works to meet the needs of all stakeholders, from the customers to the investors who purchased a few shares through a mobile app.

The board of directors usually consists of executive and non-executive directors. Executive directors are members of the management team that oversees day-to-day operations in the business. Non-executive directors do not have a direct role in day-to-day operations, but can contribute meaningfully to the trajectory of the business. These groups share a responsibility to oversee and approve key decisions within the organization as well as to act in the best interests of all shareholders.

When it comes to board composition, a balanced approach is ideal, provided regulatory and statutory requirements are met.

If the board is heavily comprised of management team members, there could be a tendency to follow historical patterns and to favor the ideas of the management team. The board must ensure the management team is capable and performing well without any conflicts of interest. Therefore, when the management team makes up a significant part of the board, accountability should not be overlooked. Checks and controls are one way to ensure accountability and eliminate conflicts of interest.

On the other hand, an entirely independent non-executive board can alienate willingness from ability when it comes to executing mandates. Those outside an organization may have a more difficult time assessing the capabilities and limitations of a day-to-day function than those who lead that function. That said, it does ensure greater accountability towards the management team when that is the case. Besides, management team members can always be invited to attend board meetings and provide clarity without having a board seat.

In that way, the board can make independent, non-biased, and well-informed decisions without sacrificing efficiency.

An organization's board of directors can also create focus groups and committees to better manage its time and workload, which streamlines decision-making and assigns specific tasks to qualified members.

Common Types of Committees

- Audit committee: Should ideally consist of independent, non-executive board members, as well as experienced finance and accounting executives, such as the chief financial officer. Among its duties are managing financial reporting and risks, internal audits, and the selection and oversight of external auditors.

- Remuneration committee: Most effective when composed mostly of independent non-executive board members to mitigate conflicts of interest, as it approves pay for executives, with at least one member well versed in remuneration structure and incentives. It advises on the remuneration framework for both the company and the board. It must also ensure the company can attract and retain high caliber executives and board members.

- Executive committee: This committee serves as the steering committee for the Board of Directors. In an ideal world, it limits the board's attention to issues that qualify as priorities, by making sure that analyses, requests, and approvals are vetted, questioned, and verified before they are submitted to the BOD for final approval. It also has the power to act on behalf of the board on certain matters. For example, if the BOD approves a C-suite level hire or replacement, the executive committee could help take the lead on hiring a suitable executive. The executive committee typically consists of senior executives from within the company as well as independent, non-executive BOD members.

In general, the board[ii] and its committees are expected to review, provide input on, and approve the following:

- The business' annual budget, along with any revisions made during the year
- Maintaining a strategic plan
- Key Performance Indicators (KPIs) for financial and operational performance
- Changes in the capital structure of the company
- Limits and controls for contracts and expenditures above a certain threshold
- The annual report of the company
- Company announcements and press releases
- Fines and penalty settlements exceeding certain limits
- Litigation settlements exceeding certain limits
- Restructuring mechanism for bad debts, if necessary
- Insurance policies acquired

- Capital expenditures in excess of predetermined limits
- The selection and hiring of key positions

Unsurprisingly, organizations with high-quality boards and committees have better governance.

Common Characteristics of an Effective Governing Body

- When the number of its members is optimal, meaning that there are no extra cooks in the kitchen who must be validated and heard. An effective governing body will only include those with something meaningful to contribute.

- When the members of the board and its committees regularly attend meetings and actively participate in important agenda items. This is more likely to occur when board materials are shared in advance, so that all members are prepared and informed, and requests for approval are supported by sufficient documentation.

- When members are held to a high standard, consistently meet expectations, and go above and beyond on their duties. Such duties include interpreting financial statements, advising on strategic expansions, and facilitating high-profile introductions and meetings. If a board member promises to meet with a regulator and get feedback on a high-priority item, they are expected to keep other members updated.

- When all members agree on the company's strategy and direction. As such, decision-making is simplified, and high-value discussion and agenda items are invited.

- When board meeting minutes and follow-up items are clearly outlined, shared with everyone, and the next meeting starts with updates on key items from the previous meeting.

- When all board and committee communication channels are respected. No surprises or shocks, or under-the-table channels are used to bypass key members of the management team (e.g., the CEO) due to lack of trust or perceived underperformance.

- When the performance of the board and its committees is continuously evaluated leading to a continuous evolution. The governance of publicly-listed companies is comparable to that of democracies. Democracies periodically evaluate their leaders. Those who do not fulfill their obligations are replaced. Even those that are performing well don't stay in power forever.

DECONSTRUCTING STRUCTURE

In an organized business environment, workload and decision-making should flow smoothly through the organization structure.

An effective structure allows the management of a company to evolve from a centralized unit for command and control, to decentralized management through delegation and empowerment of employees, coupled with clear role descriptions, responsibilities, and hierarchies.

The best organizational structures,[iii] regardless of their size, design, and requirements, enable the following:

- Flexibility to respond to changes in the external environment
- Inter-departmental collaboration and clear role accountability within departments
- Balanced risk-reward approach based on the company's dynamic risk appetite
- Growth-minded culture with a clear path to scalability

- Simplification and automation of complicated tasks
- Customer-centric design
- Clear policies, procedures, processes, and systems that are respected by all
- Performance-based culture that strives for operational excellence
- Continuous leadership development and well-crafted succession planning

Here's an example of what an organizational structure for a company could look like:

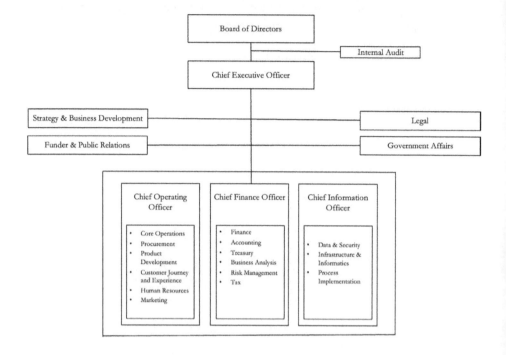

The only constant in an organization structure is in its continued evolution and adaptation to the needs of the organization.

That is because people come and go. They get promoted. They are replaced. They move on to seize new opportunities.

Business needs and operating models change. The company culture evolves. Business strategy changes.

Sometimes things simply stop working in an organization the way they once did. When an outdated organizational structure does not reflect the current state of the business, bottlenecks in decision-making and workflows are more likely to form. Therefore, a continuous evolution in the organizational structure could help incentivize management and staff to adopt and adapt.

Organizational Structure Best Practices

Dimension	Poor	Best Practice
Roles & Responsibilities	Employees are unclear about their role in the organization	Roles and responsibilities are abided by across departments
Reporting Lines	No respect for reporting lines. Loss of accountability	No breaches of reporting lines
Spans of Control	The number of direct reports is too big to properly manage across all departments	The number of reports is optimal across all departments
Interdepartmental Collaboration	No interactions between departments whatsoever	Regular cross-department meetings with structured agendas, goals, responsibilities, and follow-ups
Key Vacancies/ Missing Functions	Continuous vacancies prevalent in key roles and functions	Organization structure with all necessary functions actively staffed

Authority matrix	One-person decision-making entity. No real definition of authority matrix	Developed and disseminated authority matrix with decentralized decision making

After the organization structure is set and implemented, there needs to be an honest assessment of what is working and what could be made better until the structure is positioned for maximum functionality.

For instance, a newly established department failing to achieve its intended results, a bottleneck persisting in decision-making, or employees refusing to respect newly approved reporting lines are all issues that need urgent attention, and perhaps a rethink of the latest organizational structure.

Such changes come with opportunities that can leave stakeholders better off and render targets and business objectives more achievable.

Key Considerations

- Are the board and the management team clear on the evolution of the organization structure and the problems such an evolution would be aiming to solve? (History shows that opposition from one leader could derail an entire transformation.)

- Are there talented individuals, in key leadership and administrative positions, capable of supporting a structural transition? In other words, does the company have the right people in the right places to facilitate the adoption of a new structure?

- Are key employees aligned with regard to the proposed changes and are they clear on their level of involvement in the implementation process?

- Is the structural implementation process transparent, complete with employee input and engagement? Is there a dynamic feedback loop between leaders and employees?

AN INVISIBLE DREAM TEAM: POLICIES, PROCEDURES, PROCESSES, AND SYSTEMS

The invisible dream team referred to in the title above is not one of individuals, but rather a dream team of policies, procedures, processes, and systems, which can do wonders for an institution once they are properly implemented.

Policies are general guidelines that discuss expectations of how specific situations and issues are handled. They are the bridge between what an organization claims it stands for and how it interprets those claims on the ground. As an example, a policy may be written and enforced that ensures all employees are treated equitably and fairly. Perhaps there is a policy that ensures employees are using company resources properly and not abusing them, such as limiting business expenses on client entertainment to USD 100 per client per meeting. There can also be a policy that outlines terms and conditions for customer refunds.

A procedure maps out the steps that are taken to enforce a policy. It can also be thought of as a set of rules and standards that people follow on a day-to-day basis to make sure what is stipulated in a policy takes effect. Procedures are more specific than policies and help lay out exactly what needs to be done without leaving any room for misinterpretation. For example, if an employee is entitled to 15 paid vacation days per year, the procedure would outline the steps and conditions for obtaining required approvals.

Processes are largely defined as tools or methods that help maximize operational efficiency and productivity.[iv] A process usually articulates the steps employees need to take, as well as the way decisions and work must flow across the organizational structure to complete a certain piece of the puzzle. Each process usually pertains to a specific task in a business. Leads and prospects are converted into paying customers through the customer acquisition process. The fulfillment process might include ensuring the product is delivered to the customer at the expected time. The receivables' collection process could involve identifying receivables that have been outstanding for more than a predetermined number of days and following up with the right people to ensure that these receivables are collected and do not remain outstanding.

Systems are the entire puzzle and not just a piece of it. Systems are all about managing and optimizing institutional activities through a combination of tools, employees, and processes. The end goal of a great system is for it to do the work for you and not the other way around. Therefore, without proper systems, the business becomes overly reliant on key people. In other words, these people "become" the business.

In basketball, a system is a type of collaboration in a particular sequence according to key roles assigned to each player. Depending on the position of the player, and whether the team is on defense or offense, each member will need to move in a certain sequence and conduct a specific type of activity. As long as everyone respects and follows the "system," it will serve its intended purpose, which is to either score a basket or prevent a basket from being scored to the highest probability of success. When a particular system is called, all players know the drill and take their positions. The same applies to systems in corporations. Implementing specific processes, using necessary tools, and utilizing key people are all fundamental components.

What do you say about having a dream team play for you, while you take all the credit?

Forget about the idea that only large multinational corporations can afford to work on policies, procedures, processes, and systems.

By implementing these elements efficiently, you can boost profits, remove bottlenecks, minimize error, improve employee satisfaction, and mitigate internal and external risks.

THE RISK CANCELING EQUATION

Business leaders are regularly faced with decisions that entail risk. There is no way to completely avoid risk, but there are ways to mitigate it.

Risk management as a process can ensure that decisions are made based on best practices.[v]

A great method to manage risk is by maintaining a risk register. Developing a risk register requires brainstorming to identify and describe potential risks, investigating and estimating risk impact, defining risk owners, prioritizing risks, and creating risk response plans.

These response plans should include mitigation measures and associated costs to minimize the impact of such risks.

A risk register can also record the outcome of certain events that may have been mishandled.

It is impossible to anticipate every risk that could arise in a particular context. However, having a risk management plan in place enables businesses to respond or change course before a risk turns into a problem that can sidetrack an entire operation.

When dealing with risk, it is wise to come to the table as educated and informed as possible. This allows for the elimination of risk from risk-taking itself.

Common Risk Categories Included in a Risk Register

The following are a few examples of the various types of risks that may affect a certain company, along with some examples within each risk category.

- Strategic risks: Failing to meet strategic objectives and risk of industry disruption.

- Market risks: Loss of major clients/accounts, or outperformance by competitors.

- Financial risks: Inability to meet financial obligations and being adversely impacted by currency and interest rate fluctuations.

- Legal risks: Risk of litigation due to contract breach, risk of stricter regulations that affect the current modus operandi, and fraud risk.

- HR and IT risks: Losing high performers, having trouble hiring people, loss of data, and cyber risks.

- Operational risks: Major disasters on site, as well as environmental, health, and safety risks.

In many ways, resilience in business grows from the calculated exposure to risk rather than the complete avoidance of it.

Relevant Questions

Few questions are enough to determine whether you need to upgrade your risk management strategy:

- Do you actively pursue risk management?
- Are you able to list all potential risks you are exposed to or could be exposed to?
- Do you understand the impact of such risks?
- Do you have a mitigation strategy to keep those risks in check?

Risk management is probably not your number one priority unless you manage risks for a living.

However, it should not be underestimated or overlooked, as it may cost you much more than you anticipated.

If you strengthen your position, you will be less likely to suffer a blow from looming risks you are probably too busy to see.

Would it hurt to take your risk management framework just one notch higher?

REPORTING AS A SOURCE OF POWER

The most accurate picture of what is happening on the ground comes from business reporting. When done right, it can assist company leaders in making informed decisions based on facts and data, as well as facilitate the process of accessing funding from institutions and investors.

There is no way to overstate this: good reporting reflects the real circumstances of the business regardless of what is claimed or stated. Reports generally highlight areas of overperformance or underperformance. They point to areas of concern, trends, and areas that need urgent attention.

After all, to improve certain metrics, it is a good idea to identify them, measure them, observe the patterns and trends, and improve them accordingly.

Reporting frameworks vary depending on the capabilities and needs of the business, but the following may be considered:

- An easy-to-access dashboard for the management team that highlights key information. Essentially, this is a cheat sheet that contains all the important information and allows them to keep track of performance. Measures such as operational and financial Key Performance Indicators (KPIs) as well as a look at the pipeline of business would be helpful. Items can be arranged by importance and urgency, along with contact details for key people to contact.

- Monthly reports detailing key financial and operational metrics, along with a "management discussion and analysis" section explaining management's views. It is important that these reports follow a format that is easy to update and easy to read, so that they can be sent to the board of directors (BOD) and shareholders, if they request them. Additionally, they can be used to prepare materials for board meetings and to request board approvals.

- Reports that are more comprehensive which are issued on a quarterly, semi-annual, and annual basis. Such reports can assist with tracking historical performance, setting budgets for the months ahead, setting initiatives, as well as solidifying business and tactical plans.

Reporting Practices Checklist

- In terms of numbers, are all stakeholders on the same page?
- Do data and numbers appear consistent across departments?
- Does the company have easy-to-read, easy-to-update reporting templates?
- Is reporting integrated with the software used by the company? Where possible, has automation been considered to minimize human error?
- Does the company undergo a periodic independent review of its reports to determine their efficacy and accuracy?

WHO IS YOUR AUDITOR?

It might not be a big deal to have the company's finances audited by a well-known auditor if the company is not looking for external investment through debt, equity, or a combination of both.

However, when implementing value creation initiatives or looking for investment, the engagement of a reputable auditor to verify a company's financial records makes it easier for a company to raise funds and achieve its value-creation goals.

Parties looking to acquire or infuse capital into a business want to ensure the results and quality of earnings are representative of the risk exposure they are willing to take. The more obscure the situation, the more challenging it will be to close a deal. On the other hand, companies that can demonstrate and provide high-quality financial statements reviewed by an independent, reputable auditor, will have a much easier time raising capital.

Due to their nature of work, auditors are obligated to avoid any behavior or omissions that could harm others, especially those who rely on their reports. They are expected to highlight where a company might have weak internal controls. They are also expected to give their opinion as a function of whether they believe the company's financials represent an accurate view of the business, whether they have been provided enough access to data, and whether there could be any diversions from accounting standards.

Banks and investors ask for audited financial statements for obvious reasons. They want to ensure that there are no impediments from the beginning, that the numbers they are receiving are accurate and reliable, and that they are not acting negligently by relying on figures that could be misrepresented.

Many private businesses do not prepare audited financial statements. And that's not the end of the world. However, it is important to understand that, in the absence of financial statements audited by a reputable auditor, access to capital could get more complicated.

COMPANIES OUTLIVE GREAT LEADERS

Any decision made by a firm's leaders can impact its stakeholders, regardless of whether those decisions are good or bad. In addition to employees, other stakeholders like customers, shareholders, and even communities can also be impacted.

One of the costliest mistakes a company can make is assigning the wrong leadership to take its reins. Without a succession plan, it is more likely that ill-suited leaders will emerge.

So, what does it really mean to have a succession plan and how can succession be planned?

A succession plan is simply a process that aims to identify and develop the talent that could replace departing leadership without leaving the company worse off.

Nobody stays in a leadership position forever. Therefore, preparing for such moments will ensure the smooth passing of the torch to qualified candidates who will safeguard the company, its shareholders, its employees, its promise to its customers, and its legacy in the future.

Succession is a ubiquitous concern for a company. Pre-planned leadership transfer can ensure that the business will continue to exist and will manage to outlive the people who currently run it.[vi]

A great succession plan helps anticipate requirements ahead of time and goes to the extent of preparing certain people for leadership roles. It is about thinking ahead and equipping people with the right tools to rise to the occasion when their time comes.

You may be sitting on a gold mine of talent with your current team. Your familiarity with them does not diminish their competence. They may even be more qualified due to their understanding of the company's DNA, its culture, and its organizational dynamics.

Occasionally, however, replacements must be sought externally. That is more difficult, given that the new leaders might not have a thorough understanding of what their role entails, the company's culture, its employees, or its specifics.

Imagine that a departing CEO is replaced by a new CEO from outside the company. To get up to speed, learn about the management team and employees, and develop a rapport with the board, they will probably need at least six months. If in six months the CEO doesn't turn out to be a good fit for the role, the company will have a serious issue on its hands.

The requirements of a succession plan depend on the current standing of the company. But regardless of the specifics, it is an ongoing exercise that will continue to demand a level of strategic projection and vision by those currently in a position of power.

After all, a company cannot outlive its founders and best leaders if its successors are not the right people for the job.

Leadership Succession Checklist

- What would happen to the company if the current leadership left? What would the effects be on operations in the medium term?

- Would internal candidates be able to step up to leadership roles? How long would it take for them to become comfortable in those positions? Is training an option?

- Should the company consider hiring external candidates?

- Are there additional roles that need to be filled soon that would strengthen the organization structure and allow for a smoother transition of leadership when the time comes?

Is it hard to see how such a strategy could prove to be a lifesaver for a company that is facing a leadership crisis?

THE BUSINESS CONTINUITY PERSPECTIVE

It is often when something goes wrong in a company that we focus on corporate governance and wonder what could have been done to prevent it. Taking an active approach to corporate governance could minimize regret in such situations.

By ensuring that an organization's ecosystem runs smoothly, corporate governance safeguards its legacy. In this way, all stakeholders can reach their full potential and take responsibility for their actions. Risks relating to operations, finances, and key individuals are reduced to a minimum, enabling a business to endure.

Imagine having a clear blueprint of how all departments interact with each other, how decisions are made based on predetermined criteria, and how factors that can place the company at risk are brought to the board with objective, detailed recommendations.

Imagine how much easier it is for external lenders and prospective investors to commit funds to a company knowing there are controls and checks in place, and that the allocation of their funds is done with transparency and integrity.

Succession planning is not a concern for companies with sensible corporate governance. Even when key people leave, the show goes on. Companies such as these have pre-identified high-potential succession candidates; they have established processes to streamline leadership transitions. They have set guidelines, and they have the right people who step up in difficult situations.

There is no doubt that companies with better governance go further, stay competitive longer, and have work cultures that are equitable, effective, and thriving.

TAKE ACTION: Governance Boosting Exercise

The following is a quick questionnaire that can help you start improving your governance structure:

- Are you leveraging a class A board, with the right structure, representation, and committees? Are your board members well connected to the industry and its supporting ecosystems (e.g., suppliers, potential corporate clients, banks, and investors)?

- Is the organization structure clearly defined and robust enough to meet the needs of the business? Does it provide a seamless framework for operations and decision-making, as well as clear roles and responsibilities? Is there a disseminated authority matrix with proper delegation of responsibilities?

- Are your policies and procedures formalized and enforced? Do you have systems and processes that ensure company-wide collaboration and customer-centric fulfillment of products and services?

- Do you have the right controls in place? A system of checks and balances that is designed to reduce inefficiencies, wastage, and human error?

- Can your current system anticipate and manage risk in a way that minimizes threats to your operations? Is there an integrated risk management tool in place that acts as a repository for all risks identified?

- Do you have sound, transparent, and credible operational and financial reporting that generates consistently reliable data?

- Are you working with a reputable auditor to ensure that your financials reflect the true position of the company?

- Do you actively promote and enforce a culture of integrity, openness, transparency, and accountability?

- Are you able to leave the business and have it function at capacity without interruption? Will the right decisions be made in your absence? Have you seriously considered succession planning?

If you'd like to get the most out of this exercise, go back to each of your answers and determine how you can move forward on each bullet point by taking just one step forward. You might say, for instance, "I can't leave the business for a day without risking business interruption". Perhaps you can arrange things so that you can take a half-day off every week and let someone else handle your responsibilities. You can start with half a day and build up from there. It's as simple as that.

NUMBERS GAME

Rule No. 1: Never lose money.
Rule No. 2: Never forget rule No.1

—Warren Buffet

A business can remain in operation even without reporting a profit. It can't survive without cash, however.

One of the reasons why some companies have been successful for so long is because they always have cash on hand.

When managing and allocating their resources, they make sure cash needs are met; and if cash is not available today, then they devise a strategy to get it by the time it's needed.

This chapter will demystify the numbers game when it comes to overseeing businesses. It will clarify how the numbers flow and their applications in decision-making. It will also provide you with serious ammunition for your business judgment, from explaining financial statements and their relatedness to discussing valuation methodologies.

When you take shots based on reliable and accurate numbers, you are more likely to score a favorable business outcome.

Let's briefly note a few positive attributes of sound financial management before getting into the specifics:

- Reliable, consistent, and timely financial data reflective of the latest financial position of the company

- The ability to track and manage cash flows effectively along with a robust cash tracking mechanism

- Reduced likelihood of recurring cash shortages due to normal business requirements

- Higher likelihood of obtaining and allocating sufficient funding for growth initiatives

- Greater chances of finding hidden cash in your business

- Faster timelines and easier discussions make securing financing from banks and/or investors more likely

- A higher business valuation and higher cash flows

- A greater likelihood of creating an exit event

BECOME INTIMATE WITH YOUR FINANCIAL STATEMENTS

A business's financial statements provide an accurate picture of how it is performing and what problems it may be facing.

Understanding their components and how they work will strengthen your decision-making abilities. This information allows you to determine the impact that certain decisions have on your company's financial statements, which contribute to its valuation.[vii]

Key Financial Statements

In a nutshell, financial statements demonstrate how well a business is doing; how much it makes, how much it spends, how much it keeps, and what it owes.

Let's take a closer look at each statement.

Balance Sheet

A balance sheet provides a snapshot of the financial position of an organization at a particular moment in time. It indicates the amount of resources that a business has, how it is capitalized or funded, and whether or not the business is in a strong financial position.

A balance sheet is typically broken into three main components:

- Assets: What a company owns (machinery, cash, real estate, etc.)
- Liabilities: What a company owes (e.g., payments to suppliers, debt)
- Equity: What belongs to shareholders after liabilities are accounted for

The reason it's called a balance sheet is that it must always balance according to the following formula:

$$\text{Total Assets} = \text{Total Liabilities} + \text{Total Equity}$$

Or

$$\text{Total Equity} = \text{Total Assets} - \text{Total Liabilities}$$

As you probably already know, if a business has more liabilities than assets, it is deemed insolvent, which means that it is in distress. This may indicate that the business is unlikely to pay its financial obligations when they fall due.

Income Statement

The income statement of a company provides insights into its underlying operations: how much revenue it makes from sales, what it spends on operational costs, and what it spends on non-operational items like taxes and interest. It is also possible to determine the effectiveness of a company's management by looking at its income statement.

Income Statement Items

- Revenue or Total Sales: Revenue is the total amount of money earned from all the products and services sold in a given period. This figure indicates how large the demand for your products and services is in the markets you serve. It is also what is referred to as the "top line" of a business.

- Gross Profit: An organization's gross profit is calculated by deducting direct costs from revenue. For example, if you sell a pair of shoes for USD 200, but it costs you USD 100 to procure or make that item, your gross profit will be USD 100. The term 'direct costs' refers to costs related to making and selling products, such as raw materials. It generally excludes other costs deemed fixed or indirect that have to be incurred irrespective of the production of goods, such as administrative expenses and rent.

- Earnings before interest and taxes (EBIT): Otherwise known as Operating Income, EBIT is a measure of a business's profits generated from its core operations. It excludes items that are not regarded as core, recurring, or controlled by the business. Furthermore, it excludes items such as interest and taxes, which are addressed after the EBIT figure is calculated, and, thus, are considered to be below the EBIT line.

- Earnings before interest, taxes, depreciation, and amortization (EBITDA): A company's EBITDA represents earnings before interest, taxes, depreciation, and amortization. In the same way as EBIT, this metric excludes items that are not considered core, recurring, or controlled by the business. This figure also excludes additional non-cash charges, such as depreciation and amortization.[viii] This exclusion of non-cash charges means that these charges will be reversed or added back to EBIT. Because EBITDA does not include certain non-cash charges which do not represent actual cash leaving the company, it is a better measure for estimating cash flow than EBIT.

- Net Profit: Does the business make money after accounting for all expenses? Net profit, or income, is one of the main outputs of the income statement. It represents whatever remains after all costs have been deducted from a given period's sales. Since it appears at the bottom of the income statement, this figure is also known as the "bottom line". Businesses that are profitable are more likely to invest in growth, pay higher dividends, and have easier access to capital.

Cash Flow

One of the most reliable measures of a business's success is its cash flow statement, which shows how well a business is doing and how capable it is of moving in the direction it desires.

As the name indicates, a cash flow statement shows how much cash has entered and left an organization in a certain period, in order to determine how the company's net cash position has changed.

If you begin the year with USD 15 million in cash and end the year with USD 17 million in cash, then you have a net inflow of USD 2 million in cash in that given year.

A key output for the cash flow statement is the net change in cash.

The net change in cash figure is determined by adding the following three components:

- Cash flow from operations (CFO): CFO describes the money generated by the operations of a business over a given period. In addition to the cash it already has, a business can utilize its CFO for non-operational transactions, such as servicing debt, investing in equipment, and/or paying dividends. This figure also adds back all expenses that have a non-cash nature, such as the depreciation of equipment. CFO also helps to determine whether a company can maintain or expand its operations without resorting to banks and investors.

- Cash flow from investing (CFI): CFI pertains to inflows and outflows of cash related to long-term investments, over a specific time period. A company could have an investing cash outflow related to the acquisition of an office building or the purchase of new equipment, and an investing cash inflow related to the sale of a subsidiary.

- Cash flow from financing (CFF): CFF highlights the amount of cash flowing into or out of the company in relation to its financing structure. Key items could include, but are not limited to, taking on or repaying debt, paying dividends to shareholders, or selling shares to investors.

For any given period, below are two key formulas that apply:

- Net change in cash = CFO + CFI + CFF
- Ending cash for a given period = Starting cash for a given period + Net change in cash

Having introduced the three financial statements: the balance sheet, the income statement, and the cash flow statement, it should not appear surprising that they are all interrelated. Therefore, it is helpful to understand how these statements work, since changes to one impact the others.

By understanding the "flow" and the linkages between the financial statements, you can make better decisions. You can better determine, for example, whether a certain initiative you are considering is feasible, whether you will have enough cash to fund it, and whether you will be able to cover your scheduled payments.

There is no need to worry if certain aspects of this topic are unfamiliar to you. If this is the case, you may have overlooked hidden value in your corporate setup.

HAVE YOUR KEY FIGURES HANDY

You should be familiar with a few key financial figures before discussing business performance with a counterparty. If you appear uncertain about the key financial metrics pertaining to your business, you may invite doubt into a conversation.

When you express confidence in your numbers, you show banks, investors, and other stakeholders that you know what they are looking for, and that you speak the same language. This often leads to more fruitful discussions.

Among the key figures are:

- Sales Overview: This figure helps you understand the breakdown of your sales by product category, business segment, market, or geography. How much do you sell in a given period? What are your best sellers? On average, what do you charge per sale?

- EBITDA: This figure is quite popular in financing and valuation discussions. It gives lenders a quick idea of a business's debt-servicing ability. A business with a Debt/EBITDA ratio of 10x is considered highly indebted. It is also used in valuation discussions. When a business has an EBITDA of USD 16 million, and comparable businesses have sold for 7x EBITDA, then the implicit valuation of this business would be USD 16 million * 7 = USD 112 million. Not to worry. We will discuss valuation methodologies in detail at the end of this chapter.

- Net Profit: In a traditional context, a business that cannot tell if it's making a profit does not deserve to exist.

- Net Debt: This figure shows whether a company can pay all of its debts if they were due immediately, and how much cash would remain after paying all debts. It is calculated by adding all short-term and long-term debts, then subtracting the cash available. This result is known as net debt. It is ideal to present gross and net debt figures together.

- Free Cash Flow: The term free cash flow refers to the amount of cash a business generates in a given period. To calculate this item, non-cash charges, such as depreciation, are added back to operating profits, or EBIT. In addition, working capital investment and capital expenditure are deducted. This figure indicates how much cash can be used to service debt and how much can be distributed to shareholders. Wouldn't it be nice to know what dividends you can expect to receive from the business you've just acquired?

Mastering Financial Housekeeping

Financial housekeeping occurs behind the scenes, away from the spotlight. Maintaining consistent, up-to-date records that are accessible by the appropriate departments is crucial; and staying organized, systematic, and disciplined is essential, too.

Having a solid financial framework should ensure that the business has enough cash on hand to continue to operate and act on financial ambitions. For accurate and reliable results, the framework should be simple and user-friendly, so that it can be fed with the right inputs.

Efforts spent in that area pay off in the long run, as companies can better manage their long-term needs and secure their financial future with efficient and transparent financial housekeeping.

When everything is in order, financial housekeeping should be a source of reliability, not a burden.

Below are some advantages of proper financial housekeeping:

- You will be able to find the latest operational and financial information with ease. An example could be a geographical and item breakdown of sales, a breakdown of fixed and variable costs, or a breakdown of popular items that sell quickly and have a healthy margin versus those that have sat in inventory for a long time.

- You would be able to track monthly cash flows, which may provide insight into funding gaps that need to be addressed. Keeping track of your cash outflows and inflows will let you better predict if you are at risk of running out of cash and defaulting on payments. This gives you plenty of time to secure alternative financing options.

- You can ensure that receivables are collected on time and that delays are avoided. You can also develop a framework for handling follow-up communications and delayed payments. Whenever a client breaches their payment terms, you would want to immediately follow up and notify them. Moreover, if these actions are recurring, it may be best to limit exposure to such clients who create a drain on your cash flow.

- It allows you to estimate the amount of funding that is necessary for new initiatives. If you're trying to quantify how much investment is required, you must not only consider the investment's worthiness as a stand-alone matter, but also the funding sources that will help pay for it. Can you deploy the excess cash available into the investment you are contemplating? What external funding options are available? How long will it take for that investment to pay off?

- It reduces the time and effort spent on financing discussions. Imagine going to a bank and not having the data they need to assess your eligibility for a loan. Your financial performance, your existing debt position, and your existing cash flows are necessary at a minimum to assess whether you can service your current debt and whether you can take on more debt, as well as the risk associated with doing so. When discussing your financial data with the lender, being prepared with accurate and reliable figures could help you save time and reach a resolution quickly, which could prove invaluable during the financing process.

- It optimizes the decision-making process by integrating data between departments. As a company grows, it becomes increasingly important to ensure interdepartmental collaboration and system integration. Consider, for example, that the procurement department needs to request new inventory and the finance function needs to approve the release of funds, but the data are conflicting because their systems aren't integrated. The procurement department urges the finance department to release the funds needed to order more inventory, but finance responds with "according to policy, we are not at this point yet." A software solution could help with this issue. An Enterprise Resource Planning (ERP) system helps manage and integrate processes pertaining to several functions such as finance, human resources, and procurement.

The use of an ERP system would allow all systems across several departments to be accessed via a common interface and information to be shared and communicated more effectively. Investing in systems and tools used to require a significant upfront investment in the past. However, cloud-based software has made them more affordable and accessible.

Unlock Trapped Cash

Working capital is the difference between the money you expect to collect in the short term, such as the money you are waiting to receive from clients for services rendered, and the money you expect to pay in the short term, such as the money you need to pay suppliers for products you received.

Even though companies may have booked revenues for services rendered, until they collect the cash for those services, these revenues cannot be used to cover the cash needs of the business.

Working capital reflects a company's short-term financial health and efficiency in its operations.

We're playing a financing game here.

You are essentially funding your customers for free if you offer extended payment terms. With extended terms from suppliers, however, you are essentially getting funding for free.

As a result, when you have more receivables than payables, you are putting a cash strain on yourself, leaving you with a deficit to manage.

If it is the other way around, and you are collecting cash faster than you are paying it out, you have a window of opportunity that you could use to your advantage.[ix]

Common Current Assets and Liabilities

- Accounts receivable (a current asset): Funds that you are expecting to collect in the short term for a sale that has been recorded.

- Inventory (a current asset): Raw materials used to produce goods, in addition to the final products available for sale.

- Accounts payable (a current liability): Unpaid amounts due in the short term to vendors or suppliers for goods received or services rendered.

Here are a few quick fixes you can do right now to release some trapped cash in your business:

- Reduce the amount of time it takes to collect payments from customers. Consider giving discounts as an incentive for early payment.

- Extend the time needed to pay suppliers, relative to where you are today.

- Try to negotiate better terms with new suppliers if you cannot get them from your existing ones.

- Offer discounts on inventory that has been stagnant and reinvest proceeds into products that sell faster.

Avoid The Cost-Cutting Obsession

This is not to say that having a lean cost structure isn't desirable. Often, however, we tend to focus on reducing costs to solve our cash problems, just because seeing and identifying costs is easier than identifying new revenue streams and monetizing them.

Of course, it makes sense to trim the excess fat in your cost structure, but you don't want to do so at the expense of the wellbeing of your employees, your clients, and your business.

Moreover, cutting costs cannot continue indefinitely.

When revenues increase, however, the potential for creating breathing room and bringing in more cash increases.

So, what is the right approach?

In many cases, it involves both revenue generation and cost reduction.

In order to accomplish this, a number of factors must be considered, such as the business model, the current economic environment, the leadership, as well as the ability to implement intended initiatives and strategies.

Ideas to Boost Profits

- Think of ways to sell more of what you have to offer. Maintain a customer retention program to keep existing customers who provide repeat business happy and implement creative customer acquisition strategies to attract qualified prospects to your business. Try to upsell premium products to existing customers and sell small to prospective customers. Launch innovative products to meet market needs at a healthy profit margin. Identify new revenue streams and sales channels that can be utilized. By increasing sales, more resources can be devoted to managing the business and more capital can be invested in its growth.

- The next relatively simple idea is to increase prices. If you haven't raised your prices in a long time and your costs have increased due to inflation and currency fluctuations, for example, a price increase is especially justified. You may also find that your customers are not sensitive to price changes if you have a unique position in your market. In essence, revenues are determined by price and sales volume. As a result, you will see a performance boost in your revenues and profitability if you raise your prices without affecting sales volume.

- Invest time and energy into making things more efficient. Is bureaucracy hindering the company's productivity? Do employees feel engaged enough to reach their full potential? Are there ways to generate more output without changing the inputs? Are there ways to eliminate wasted resources?

- Eliminate unnecessary and outdated expenses by following the money. Get your team together and study your cash outflows closely to see where the money is going. Examine outflows that no longer make sense for your company. Perhaps you are paying monthly fees for software that you no longer use. Determine what steps and actions you need to take to prevent further cash leakage.

FUNDING OUTSIDE THE BOX

You can raise capital for your business by taking out loans or selling shares.

An organization's capital structure describes the combination of debt and equity instruments used to finance its assets and operations in the long run. Rather than providing short-term funding, a capital structure is intended to support growth over the long term.

Based on its profile, needs, and available financing options, a company's debt and equity mix may differ.

Businesses may sometimes be financed entirely by equity, where shareholders inject cash into the company or raise investment from external investors in order to avoid taking on debt. It is possible that they do not want to borrow money or might not be able to do so, which may occur when the perceived risk of the business exceeds the funding party's tolerance for risk.

Alternatively, some owners opt to take on debt if that option is available.

There is an incentive to take on debt because interest payments are tax deductible. Choosing debt over equity also provides an incentive to keep control of the company. More investors could result in a reduction of control for the initial shareholders since more parties will be looking out for their interests.

Debt is a type of obligation in which a business must pay a predetermined interest rate and principal amount, regardless of its financial performance, or else it is considered to be in default.

By raising equity, an organization transfers ownership to its shareholders, and dividends are discretionary, meaning they are paid only when the business can afford to do so. If, for example, the company needs the cash it is generating to fund its growth plans, it can decide not to pay dividends. It may also be possible for a company to avoid paying dividends when there isn't enough cash flow available due to poor performance.

Shareholders deal with higher levels of uncertainty and risk than lenders, which is why they expect a higher return on investment.

The Dual Power of Debt

If you finance an acquisition with debt, whether it is real estate, an operating business, or just about any asset you may want to purchase, the debt you take will act as an amplifier for your position.

This means that your gains will be magnified if you are lucky and do well. This also means that you will suffer higher losses if you experience a downturn or inconvenience.

While this may seem obvious, taking on a position through an amplifier or through leverage can have serious consequences in the event of a misallocation. Losing positions will not keep you in the game for very long, especially if they are amplified, hence the need for caution.

Let's look at the example below.

Consider a scenario where you purchase a house for USD 1,000,000 by investing 20% of the total consideration from your own funds and borrowing the remaining 80% from the bank. Therefore, at the time of purchase, your own investment is USD 200,000, while the bank provides you with USD 800,000.

Say, for purposes of illustration, that the next day someone offered you USD 1,100,000 for the house, and that you were eager to sell it. Let us also assume, for simplicity's sake, that there are no other costs associated with the sale besides the settlement of debts owed.

As a result of the price increase to USD 1,100,000, the additional USD 100,000 will not be divided according to the mix of equity (20%) and debt (80%) you used for the acquisition. Instead, you will receive the entire upside. Therefore, even though the price of the house went up by 10% to USD 1,100,000, because you used debt as a funding source and an amplifier, the return on your own money invested is much higher than 10%. You would have invested USD 200,000 and ended up with USD 300,000, after paying back the USD 800,000 loan to the bank.

When a loss occurs, the same dynamic applies.

In other words, if that house lost 10% in value the next day, and you had to sell it for USD 900,000 due to personal reasons, you would still owe the bank USD 800,000. In the end, you would be left with just USD 100,000 after the sale, assuming no further penalties were imposed.

In summary, debt works in both directions when you use it to finance your positions. By understanding this dynamic, you can make better decisions based on your perception of your willingness and ability to take such risks.[x]

Here are a few questions to consider when in doubt:

- Is it okay for me to assume the entire exposure of the transaction and not just the down payment?

- Do I realize that regardless of the outcome of my assumed position, I will still be responsible for the full amount of the debt, plus interest, and other costs?

- Do I believe that the value of my acquisition today will increase at a rate greater than the interest?

Alternative Financing

So far, we have discussed the two methods companies can use to raise money: debt financing and equity financing.

A business can also raise funds by selling existing assets, such as real estate.

It might be smart for an average business to have a backup security, such as real estate. However, a successful business might incur a higher opportunity cost by adopting such a strategy.

An even more profitable strategy would be to free up capital locked in real estate assets, lease those assets back from the new party who acquires them, and reinvest that capital from the sale into business operations and growth.

An important caveat here is that the investment needs to yield returns that are better than what holding the real estate asset would offer, and with a good probability of success.

Freeing Up Capital Locked in Real Estate

Imagine you are the owner of a highly reputable and privately owned hospital that happens to own the property in which it operates.

During the most recent management meeting, the finance director discussed the hospital's latest financial position. It turns out that over the past eight months, many surgeries have been put on hold due to an ongoing pandemic, which is taking much longer than expected. As a result, the hospital's cash generation capabilities have deteriorated.

The hospital needs to raise USD 10 million over the next 100 days to continue paying star surgeons, settle debts that would become due, and ensure the patient experience and quality of care remain intact.

There is already significant unsecured debt on the hospital's books, so there is no room to take on more debt from the banks.

Although you have already explored obtaining external investment, the interested parties are your competitors, and you are reluctant to open your books and provide them with all your information. Besides, they could still walk away from a deal if they don't sign a legally binding agreement after they complete their study of the business.

According to the hospital's finance director, a sale and leaseback is the best option at this time.

A real estate investor will buy the hospital's real estate and lease it back to you, the seller. The hospital will continue to operate as usual except that the real estate will now be owned by the real estate investor. Upon signing a new lease agreement, the investor will be entitled to receive rent payments.

So, let's say the property is valued at USD 10 million, and the rental yield agreed upon in the lease is 5%. As a tenant of the real estate you've just sold to the investor, you will start paying them USD 500,000 a year in rent.

Using the USD 10 million from the proceeds of the deal, you will pay your rent, settle your bank debts, pay your star medical staff, and eventually restore full operations to the hospital.

Additionally, you will be able to earmark funds for whatever growth initiatives you wish to implement, without having to obtain debt financing or bring new investors onboard.

If you choose, you can also negotiate a buy-back option with the new investor.

That way, you will have the option of acquiring your real estate back, if you choose to do so, using a predetermined pricing mechanism, such as comparable market data at the time of the buyback.

In conclusion, using creative and alternative methods of financing can sometimes strengthen your hand by giving you cards you didn't know you had.

KNOW YOUR WORTH

Among the most popular skills sought by leaders and executives around the world is knowing how to value a business.

Wouldn't you want to know the implications of your actions if they had a direct bearing on the share price of a publicly traded company?

With a proper understanding of what drives value in a company's operations, decisions such as entering new markets, launching new products, investing in new equipment, or even acquiring a competing company become more carefully considered.

Business valuation generally refers to the present value of the operations and cash flows of a business.

There is no single gold standard for valuing a business, so companies use multiple methods that combine theory and data.

Many of these approaches are subjective, depending on the beholder's judgment and their eye for business.

In other words, it is not unusual for an acquisition deal to fail because valuation expectations between a buyer and a seller are too far apart.

COMMON VALUATION METHODOLOGIES

Discounted Cash Flow (DCF) Analysis

This method views companies as generators of future cash flows to determine what these future cash flows are worth today, using precise assumptions to estimate and discount these future cash flows back to their present value.

For example, if free cash flow in 2 years is USD 10,000,000, with a discount factor of 0.9, then that cash flow would be worth USD 9,000,000 today.

A cost of capital, which factors in the time value of money, as well as risk premiums, is approximated to determine the discount factor.

The further into the future a cash flow goes and the greater the perceived risk, the greater the discount factor.

Due to the assumptions that are incorporated into this method, DCFs can be quite complicated, but the concept itself is quite simple, and that is determining the present value of a company's future cash flows.

I recommend doing a quick search online for more information on how to build and use a DCF since there is no shortage of quality content available. Remember, though, that a DCF always determines Enterprise Value, so you will need to adjust that figure to obtain Equity Value, which is the value in a company that belongs to shareholders (more on this later in this section).

Comparable Company Analysis

Using this methodology, a relative valuation is used to determine the value of the company. It applies metrics of companies of similar size, operating in the same industry, and in similar markets and jurisdictions, to certain financial figures in the underlying business. Do not worry, this method is easier than it appears to be.

A company's trading metrics, including its price-to-earnings ratio, can be easily determined if it is publicly traded. By applying the trading metrics of comparable companies to your financial figures, you can get an indication of your valuation.

For instance, let's assume that you identify Company X, which is publicly traded, as a comparable company to yours. Let's say it trades at a P/E multiple of 20x, and that your net profit is USD 1 million. Using the comparable company method, simply multiply the P/E multiple of 20x with your net profit or earnings of USD 1 million, to get to a valuation of USD 20 million. In this case, we assume that the business being valued has no debt or excess cash, otherwise such figures would need to be accounted for in the valuation adjustments.

Also, you may apply certain discounts to the trading multiples being used, such as size, scale, or illiquidity discounts, if the company being valued is substantially smaller or not entirely similar to the public company deemed comparable.

Precedent Transactions

This method uses recent market transactions as benchmarks for evaluating a company's value.

A simple illustration of this method would be in residential real estate, where a recent house sale in a certain area is referred to in a current negotiation in the same area.

To be as accurate as possible, try to find companies that are in a similar condition to yours that have been sold recently, and apply the implied multiples of that deal, such as the price-to-earnings ratio, to your financial metrics to get an indication of your valuation.

Returns-Based Valuation

By using this technique, you can reverse engineer a valuation based on certain assumptions.

Using a 6% rental yield and knowing that an average four-bedroom house is renting for USD 6,000 per month in a given location, one can determine the value of their four-bedroom house to be USD 1,200,000 in that same location.

To get to USD 1,200,000, simply divide the annual rent of USD 72,000 by the rental yield of 6%.

Similarly, an operating company can derive a valuation from its business plan by using its target internal rate of return (IRR).

This method requires you to answer the following question: "If I were to achieve my target return based on my business plan and a set of assumptions that I am comfortable with, what should be my entry valuation, or the price I need to pay, for the business today?"

To further simplify, how much would it cost me today to acquire a property that generates USD 72,000 in annual rental income at a 6% annual rental return? The answer is USD 1,200,000.

Balance Sheet Method

Using the balance sheet is another way to value a business.

The way it works is you subtract all the liabilities from the assets of the company to arrive at the equity value as per the latest balance sheet.

This method is not the most reliable or popular, however, because the assets on the balance sheet may not be reflective of their current value. For example, a building acquired 20 years ago could be worth substantially more today than its historical acquisition cost.

To overcome this limitation, and to limit the risk of undervaluing the company, assets that are recorded at their historical values need to be assessed for their current fair market value.

Although this method has limitations, a struggling company with valuable assets could use it to justify a higher valuation based on its assets rather than its financial performance.

Liquidation Value

The liquidation value of a company is the amount of cash retained by its shareholders in the event that it has to close urgently, sell all its assets at a steep discount, and settle all its liabilities.

ADDITIONAL VALUATION CONSIDERATIONS

Now that we've covered a few methods for valuing a business, let's consider common valuation[xi] adjustments you may need to make based on the specifics of the business being valued.

Among these adjustments is a debt adjustment.

If you were the rightful owner of a USD 1,000,000 house but had a USD 500,000 mortgage on it, what would the value of your home be?

Even if you sold it today for USD 1,000,000, the proceeds wouldn't be yours entirely since you still owe money on your mortgage. You must settle the USD 500,000 debt first, then keep any remaining funds after the loan is paid off.

Therefore, the value of your ownership in the house at the time of sale is USD 500,000.

When an asset is sold, the equity value is what is left for the owner after the liabilities are settled.

Important Distinction between Enterprise Value and Equity Value

There are differences between the total valuation of an asset and the shareholder value of that asset. This is illustrated in the earlier example of the house that sold but still had a mortgage due.

When valuing an operating business, enterprise value is the total value of the business regardless of its capital structure, for instance how much debt it has, whereas equity value is the value to be attributed to its shareholders.

There are often other factors to consider, which we assume to be zero for the purpose of this section, such as items on the balance sheet deemed debt-like, minority interest, and noncontrolled assets, but the basic formula is as follows:

- Enterprise Value = Equity Value + Debt – Cash

Or

- Equity value = Enterprise Value – Debt + Cash

Please note the above section is a simplification to ensure understanding for the layperson and does not constitute financial advice. A more accurate representation of the above formula would be Equity Value = Enterprise Value - Debt and Debt Equivalents - Minority Interest + Non-core and Non-controlled Assets + Cash and Cash Equivalents. To obtain a more precise business valuation, you must consult with a professional who is familiar with your business operations.

FROM PRIVATE TO PUBLIC VIA IPO

The process of listing a private company on a stock exchange and offering its shares for sale to the public is known as an initial public offering (IPO).

A company may be able to reach a wider pool of potential investors through an IPO, provided it meets certain requirements to qualify for a listing.

Unlike private investment, which tends to be difficult to monetize when a shareholder needs to sell their shares, public companies allow investors to purchase and sell shares at their discretion.

In general, public companies tend to fetch a higher valuation than their privately owned counterparts, since they tend to be more liquid.

To go public, a company must follow a certain process, which varies depending on its size, financial status, and the exchange of choice. A separate discussion needs to be had about the listing process and a company's readiness for that. The main idea here is to highlight this option and argue why it could be transformational for a business.

Pros and Cons of Going Public

Depending on your circumstances, below are a few pros and cons[xii] of publicly listing your company:

Pros:

- By selling shares to a wider pool of investors, you can raise more capital.

- As opposed to investing in private companies, you provide investors with liquidity, allowing them to buy and sell shares faster through an exchange.

- You can use your stock as currency to merge with or acquire other businesses.

- Talent becomes easier to attract. Brand recognition will increase, and you can use your stock to offer incentives and pay appropriately.

- Publicity and prestige will increase. In this way, you can gain recognition within your ecosystem and better manage your reputation in the market.

- Improved negotiating position with vendors and suppliers.

Cons:

- A degree of complexity. Going public requires significant preparation and compliance with specific regulations.

- Offering ownership to strangers, potentially.

- A loss of control. Some management decisions will require shareholder approval.

- Public disclosure requirements, including sharing financial reports.

- It is necessary to maintain relationships with shareholders and to respond to their concerns.

- Performance could affect share price, so there is more pressure to deliver.

- You will need to hire external advisors and consultants; going public is expensive, and you must secure a budget to fund the process.

CLOSING REMARKS ON THE NUMERICAL HOCUS POCUS

I understand that this chapter has gotten a little technical and that numbers and equations aren't the most exciting topics.

You might, however, have noticed areas that could be useful for your business setup. Please do not disregard those areas. You would be doing yourself a disservice if you do.

This chapter's key takeaway can be summarized as follows: Every business needs a structured system for managing its finances and allocating its resources. A robust financial framework will result in improved cash flows, higher valuations, and more resilient businesses.

I'd like to remind you of some important things we discussed in this chapter:

- Understanding the three financial statements, how they work, and how they are interrelated

- Understanding what working capital is, and how it can be utilized in an advantageous manner

- Keeping your financial house in order by having the right mindset and leveraging technology (example: using an enterprise resource planning system)

- Understanding the pros and cons of utilizing debt and equity as sources of financing

- The dual power of debt and its role as an amplifier

- Assessing alternate sources of funding (a sale-leaseback structure, for example)

- Common valuation methodologies and key considerations and adjustments when valuing companies

- Examining the pros and cons of listing a company on a stock exchange to obtain funding and raise the company's profile

Having a firm grasp of the financial figures and how they interact with each other is a superpower, and a solid understanding of strategic finance can significantly boost the chances of transforming your business.

TAKE ACTION: Cash Boosting Exercise

To boost profits and improve cash flow generation, consider the following:

- Analyze the revenue buildup of the business in detail. If possible, separate revenue streams by client and product. Assess the profit margins and sales volumes of your key products. Check that your clients are paying you in accordance with the terms you agreed to and that you have collected everything that is owed to you.

- Conduct a deep dive into leakages in the business by scheduling a meeting with key finance and accounting management. Consider measures that might positively impact the cash position and profitability of the company. For example, identify subscriptions to software or recurring payments the organization no longer needs, then stop renewing them.

- Speak with your tax advisor about any items that might be tax deductible, or which potentially qualify as a business expense, so that you can reduce your tax burden.

- Consider alternative sources of funding, such as the liquidation of old inventory or the sale-and-leaseback of fixed assets. It's not always easy to obtain debt at favorable terms, nor is it always the preferred method of raising cash. Many financial experts recommend not exceeding a Debt/EBITDA ratio of 5x.

- Establish your normalized levels of working capital to make sure your business operations are never disrupted. Check if you can negotiate more favorable terms with your suppliers to reduce your working capital cycle, i.e., the time it takes to convert your working capital, which is calculated as current assets minus (-) current liabilities, into hard cash. Consider offering your customers a cash discount if they pay you earlier than they normally would.

- Assess capital expenditure needs based on a clear return on investment (ROI) framework. For instance, only invest in equipment that generates a minimum ROI of 33%, which implies a three-year payback period.

- Take advantage of existing banking relationships to access new financial solutions and reduce borrowing costs. It is important to remember that debt carries a tax shield, which offsets interest expense.

- Assess your company's readiness for an IPO if appropriate and prepare accordingly. If necessary, reach out to advisors for more clarity on the process. Initial consultations are usually free.

Exercises of this type usually yield quick results, especially when you do them for the first time. Take this opportunity to get started and see what happens!

BULLETPROOF STRATEGY

Strategy without tactics is the slowest route to victory.
Tactics without strategy is the noise before defeat.

—Sun Tzu

A business must continuously add value to its market in order to remain viable.

When a business excels at corporate strategy, it is well-aware of who it is, its position in the market, and its goals for the future.

An organization's strategic direction aligns its goals with its resources, in order to improve what is, as well as to plan for what may become.

Its employees are engaged, and their attitudes indicate a sense of ownership and responsibility toward their roles and the direction they are taking.

Milestones and goals are more easily attained, and the overall focus is on the things that matter.

Day-to-day operations are optimized and there is minimal resource wastage.

In addition, stakeholders operate with conviction, a strong sense of direction, and a collaborative attitude.

Consequently, the company is better able to sustain the creation of value in its market. The business judgment of its stakeholders becomes more accurate and more in line with reality, and more favorable outcomes arise from the right decisions.

I think the insights in this section will serve your business strategy, so don't stop reading just yet, because they are sure to add value to your efforts.

Below is a sample of what we will be talking about and addressing in this chapter:

- What effect do market forces have on us? How well-positioned are we to withstand market shocks? What criteria should we use to evaluate market conditions?

- Are we accurate in our assessment of the business's current state? Do we have a strategic and tactical plan that is both ambitious and realistic? Are we on track for this year's budget?

- Would we like to improve our products and services? Do we plan to introduce new products?

- How will we innovate within our existing markets? Are we planning on entering new markets?

- Is there a pricing strategy in place?

- Are we leveraging the latest technological advancements within our industry?

- Is it possible to remain relevant in an industry that is under constant technological disruption?

- Are we intentional in the way we manage our culture? Do employees agree with our assessment?

- Is our brand strategy well thought out?

- Would we be open to joint ventures (JVs) and strategic partnerships? Are we open to mergers and acquisitions (M&A)?

TAMING THE MARKET FORCES

With all its assets, operations, and stakeholders, a business is an entire ecosystem of its own that impacts all those who serve it and are served by it: the employees, the management team, the board, the shareholders, the customers, the creditors, the suppliers, even communities that have nothing to do with the business!

It is also an ecosystem within a larger ecosystem that is more complex and not directly controlled by a business's key stakeholders or influencers: the market in which it operates.

The forces that affect the market and the industry aren't to be played with or ignored no matter how good you are at running your business. This is because the impact of these forces can often be quite significant.

Understanding these forces, as well as adopting strategies around them, will benefit companies' ecosystems as well as strengthen their position in the markets they wish to penetrate and operate in.

Now let's look at these forces.

MARKET FORCES

Supply

To understand how this force works, you need to be aware of what is happening in your market.

For example, you will have a significant advantage if you are able to determine who else is competing with you for market share today, and whether additional, more sophisticated competitors will emerge tomorrow.

Read the news, set up Google alerts, stay up to date, attend trade conferences if relevant, and network in your industry and in your market of interest. Being aware of the tactics and strategies your competitors are adopting is imperative to your understanding of how this force is evolving over time.

Demand

How big is the current market for your industry? Is there any indication that the market will grow in the future? What are the key factors that drive demand for your products?

Market demand is reflected in your answer to any of the questions above. In the absence of demand for a product, there is no market for it.

Would you be able to create demand for your product in a market that is currently untapped?

Would you be able to sustain demand for your products in a market that is being disrupted by technology? Will you be able to pivot in order to stay relevant and profitable?

If you want to calculate the market size in a given year, or the demand within a particular market, you can use the formula below:

Market demand = (# of customers in a given market) multiplied by (average price per product) multiplied by (# of products purchased in a given year).

If you cannot locate the above statistics, consider identifying a publicly traded company that you deem relevant in your market of interest. The annual reports of such companies often contain information about the market. A public company's annual report can typically be found in the "Investor Relations" section of its website.

Regulation

In all industries, companies are regulated by various types of government and regulatory agencies. In addition to licensing requirements, business conduct requirements, entry barriers, environment regulations, and safety regulations, these bodies and agencies have a great deal of influence over businesses. Among these agencies are the SEC, the Health Department, and the Environmental Protection Agency.

Safety regulations are among the most critical in all industries. For example, if you run a hospital without a clear escape route in case of a fire, you might not be able to schedule surgery patients on floors where the floor plans do not meet certain fire evacuation standards. To obtain necessary approvals, you might be required to tear down some walls and create the necessary space for the safe and prompt evacuation of patients in the event of a fire.

During certain situations, such as a pandemic, regulators may also dictate when you can open and what percentage of your capacity you can utilize.

In all aspects of business, regulation must be considered. There is no escaping it.

The following are some key questions to consider regarding regulations:

- What is the level of regulatory complexity in a particular industry? What does it look like?

- How familiar are you with all the different regulatory bodies involved? What are their requirements, procedures, and timelines like?

- Are there any anticipated changes to regulation that could have a direct impact on the business? In what ways? What could be done to mitigate such risks?

Manpower

If you're planning to run a large business, you'll probably need employees.

This force is all about being able to hire the right talent in your desired market.

- Is the talent supply sufficient to meet the market's needs?

- Will you be able to hire tech talent for the startup you're building?

- Are there any visa restrictions that would hinder access to international markets in the event of a talent shortage?

- Would you be able to hire professionals (such as nurses, GPs) locally if you opened a 100-bed hospital in a remote area?

- Are you going to be able to hire teachers who have the right credentials for the special needs center you plan to open?

- Does the difficulty of retaining and hiring talent limit your growth?

To conclude on this topic, leaders, influencers within an organization, as well as other internal and external stakeholders should always keep an eye on market forces such as supply, demand, regulation, and manpower.[xiii]

The effects they can have on businesses and entire industries are simply too great to ignore.

There is constant change in markets. An announcement of a new law could happen at any moment. Another possibility is that a massive competitor may enter your market and tap into your employees and customers with better deals, just when you thought things were under control. This kind of competitor might even be able to operate at a loss until they secure their position in their new market.

It is up to visionary leaders to pick up on these developments and navigate complex situations wittingly.

You could be doing a phenomenal job internally and still get wiped out by these external factors. They could also take care of a lot of things for you, and act in your favor, if you are well acquainted with them.

All About Benchmarking

It might sound controversial, but businesses in a competitive market compete almost as if they are at war with one another. In fact, there will always be a war between businesses vying for a certain market.

They strategize to use their resources effectively so that they can capture as much market share as possible.

They aim to make sure they don't leave anything on the table for their competitors.

These companies have powerful in-house legal teams and have no hesitation in hiring external attorneys if they feel their rights have been infringed upon by competitors.

To entice qualified "fighters" to join their "army" or workforce, they pay them wages that motivate them to join. And depending on the market conditions, they might even offer some ridiculous incentives in order to attract the best talent on the market.

At the end of the day, what do they hope to accomplish? Getting your money! Capturing as much of the market as possible. That's their ultimate motive.

Competition Analysis Checklist

Map out the market and its constituents

- How would you describe your target market? What are its demographics?

- Do you know the key players in your target market that compete with you for business?

- Who will likely compete with you in the future?

Compare Yourself to Competitors

Identify the competition and assess your competitors based on the following parameters:

- How well can you compete with them?

- What is your current estimated market share relative to theirs?

- How do their key operational and financial metrics compare to yours? Some of these items might include capacity, utilization, product portfolio, number of employees, revenues, profitability, and debt.

- How long have your competitors been in business, and who are their key customers?

- Which sales channels do they use and what are their pricing models?

- Who are their investors, board members, star employees, and key customers?

- What are they better at than you? Is their innovation superior to yours?

- How do they appear to the market? Does their brand stand out?

- Do they have alliances and ties with other companies that give them an edge?

As long as you intend to stay in the game, you're going to need to strategize to cement your position in your desired marketplace. Getting to know your market and the key players serving it is essential to being a strong contender in that territory.

BUDGETING AND PLANNING IN THE AGE OF DISRUPTION

It is much easier to get to where you're going if you have a map, especially if you're visiting for the first time.

Having a concise, clear, and comprehensive plan can give your strategy all the ammunition it needs to succeed.

There are many examples of great ideas that failed simply because they were never executed properly.

In order to realize their visions, companies invest in their strategic plans, their budgets, and their tactical plans.

Their vision and intent can be broken down into clear and actionable steps, with clear deadlines. They can delegate important tasks to those who are most likely to succeed at implementing them.

As a result, such actions invite ambitious, yet realistic, discussions about what is feasible today and what might be possible tomorrow.

Budgets and business plans provide a clear sense of direction in an operating business. They help outline the key milestones and actions necessary to realize the business's objectives within a certain period of time.[xiv]

Budget vs. Business Plan

Although both documents include a financial forecast and are forward-looking, there are a few key differences between a budget and a business plan.

- Duration: Budgets are usually conducted over a shorter period, around 12 months at the latest, whereas business plans have a medium- to long-term focus, typically between three and five years.

- Scope and depth: Budgets generally include an itemized list of various revenue and cost items. In a business plan, a more generalized view is presented, together with market data, commercial information, and a strategy for the next few years.

Achievable Budget Considerations

Consider the following questions when creating an ambitious yet achievable budget:

- Do you have a sales target? Can you increase prices without dampening demand?

- How will resources be allocated across departments and key initiatives?

- Do you expect the prices of key raw materials to increase? Will there be any cost savings for your company?

- Are you considering raising salaries for your key staff members? Is it likely that you will need to hire more people to support your pipeline and plans?

- How do administrative costs look? Will you renegotiate leases that are up for renewal?

- Do you have a marketing strategy?

- What is your goal in terms of profitability?

- Are there any short-term initiatives you need to succeed at in order to maximize your chances of achieving your budget? What is your projected net income? Do you intend to pay dividends?

- Do key people agree with your proposed targets? Can they see the value in your suggestions? How clear are the lines of accountability and responsibility in your organization?

Triumphant Business Plan Considerations

To build a triumphant business plan, consider incorporating the following viewpoints:

- Where does the business stand today? In what direction do you intend to take it? How do you intend to accomplish that?

- Are you planning to enter new markets? What will the process look like? How will these markets contribute to your business over the next three to five years?

- What is the target revenue contribution you expect from existing and new products/services, branches, jurisdictions, and offices?

- Would you consider adding third-party partnerships or online sales channels to your business strategy?

- What changes will you make to your cost structure? Could you realize any cost efficiencies?

- How are you going to develop your marketing strategy? How is your acquisition cost per customer evolving?

- How are you going to manage your working capital? Will you require working capital financing? Can you reduce the working capital cycle?

- Are you planning to invest in fixed assets to support business growth? Do you intend to take on external financing to support your expansion plans?

- Do you have the right leadership in place for the duration of the business plan? Are there any positions that you will need to hire externally?

- Are you providing any incentives to key management and employees? In what way will they be rewarded if your targets are met?

- Would you consider acquiring any businesses to add to your offering of products/services? Could acquiring certain businesses help you expand into other markets faster?

- Over the next few years, what will be your sources of funding? Does the business produce enough cash to support the investments you will need to make?

- Is external funding required? If so, what amount can you raise from banks? Can you raise money from investors as well?

As business plans span a number of years and are, in most cases, dependent on the base year, you need to focus on getting your first year right, which stems from your budget.

Therefore, your budget needs to be as realistic and achievable as possible.

Consider your business plan unlikely to hold up in the event of a poor first-year performance.

Imagine you are aiming to generate USD 20 million in sales in year one as per your budget and forecasting a 10% increase in the next year, which is USD 22 million in sales. Your projection of USD 22 million for year two is unlikely to hold if you only generate USD 13 million in year one, rather than the USD 20 million you budgeted. The same is true for subsequent years.

Financial partners and investors usually request both documents: the budget and the business plan. The quality of your documents makes an excellent impression on anyone assessing the opportunities your company offers, especially if you can show a solid track record of meeting or exceeding your goals in the past. Furthermore, they show that thought and effort have been invested into setting the business and its stakeholders on an appropriate path.

To Sell or Not to Sell

Marketing is all about getting the right information in front of the right audience to generate sales-ready traffic.

Prior to modern marketing, identifying and contacting the "right audience" was much more challenging. Nowadays, however, there is access to a vast amount of data which can be processed by numerous media channels and sites, ensuring that you reach your target audience.

Let's not fool ourselves. There's a reason companies pay prime dollars for advertisements. They're confident that their advertising spend will produce the return on investment they are seeking.

TAKE ACTION: Develop Effective Marketing and Sales Strategies

Marketing and sales go hand in hand. They are two sides of the same coin.

While marketing focuses on generating interest in your company and what you have to offer, selling focuses on monetizing that interest.

Effective Marketing

- Define your ideal customer as precisely as you can

- Be as specific as possible when describing the problem you are trying to solve

- Understand your customers' pain points to position a product that meets their needs

- Demonstrate the value, benefit, or experience your product or service will provide

- Diversify your sources of traffic to reduce dependence and concentration risks (e.g., TV commercials, specialized magazines, Google ads, Facebook ads, LinkedIn ads)

- Familiarize yourself and continuously monitor your key marketing metrics, such as acquisition cost per customer, lifetime value per customer, and return on advertising spend (ROAS)

Effective Sales

- Consider offering a low-risk, low-priced, or free item to reduce initial buyer resistance and skepticism, and then build buyer-seller relationships (example: free samples or free trials)

- Study your offering's perceived value, and continually enhance it

- Establish credibility by relying on facts (example: 73% of our customers choose this model which has a 97% satisfaction rate after purchase)

- Communicate with conviction and transparency while supporting your claims with evidence

- Design a compelling offer with the right guarantees

- Increase average transaction size by presenting up-selling opportunities or bundles

- Multiply your sales channels (for example, direct sales, retail, wholesale, and eCommerce)

- Make sure your customer's journey is optimized for success. The buying process should be easy and enjoyable for your customers

- Maintain healthy relationships with customers since repeat business requires less effort and less investment than new business

Marketing → lead generation → filter for qualified prospects → convert prospects to customers → nurture relationships for repeat business[xv]

BUILDING AND PRICING FOR PROFIT

Your products and services are the means by which you deliver and realize value in your market.

As such, they are an extension of your company, your brand, and what you represent.

Having a product strategy is all about knowing the problems you are solving and mastering the design and delivery of your proposed solutions.

You should also thoroughly understand your potential customers and their profile: who they are, what their tastes are, their concerns, what they want, need, desire, their limitations, the source and nature of their skepticism, excitement, and their fears.

To sell well, your products should be more than just outputs of what you're good at or excited about. They should be tailored to what your market wants or needs. They can also be tailored to the needs your market might have in the future, even though it may not know what it needs yet. A combination of the two would be most beneficial.[xvi]

Product Strategy Considerations

- What are the key problems you are trying to solve in the market? Is there a need or desire for such solutions?

- How would you describe the profile of your target customer? Why should they be interested in what you have to offer?

- How would you describe your Unique Selling Proposition (USP)? What makes your products stand out? Are they superior to those of your competitors? Are they more visually appealing?

- Can you continuously measure the performance of your product portfolio and reallocate resources to your star products?

- Do you continuously collect feedback on your products?

- Can you demonstrate confidence in your products by offering warranties?

Once you have given enough thought to the above, consider the following:

- To ensure the quality and consistency of your products, what measures can you take?

- How can you further innovate and develop your existing product line?

- Are there any opportunities to extend your product suite by introducing new products on the market? If yes, you may want to consider the framework below:

- *Step 1: Design new product*
- *Step 2: Build minimum viable product (MVP) with basic qualifications*
- *Step 3: Collect feedback on your MVP*
- *Step 4: If feedback is encouraging, develop product further*
- *Step 5: Test product (ensure it meets quality standards)*
- *Step 6: Produce in small batches and roll out to market*
- *Step 7: Collect feedback from customers*
- *Step 8: Revisit design*
- *Step 9: Implement feedback and modify product*
- *Step 10: Test again (ensure it meets quality standards)*
- *Step 11: Produce in larger batches and sell on the market*

The Almighty Dollar

It may seem like your customers are extremely sensitive to the prices you charge them, and that they do business with you because you are cheaper than your competitors.

This might be true in a market with no clear differentiation between competitors.

But in many cases, this is a limiting belief. And the reason for that limitation is likely the lack of a pricing strategy.

Essentially, a pricing strategy refers to the methodology used to figure out how and what to charge for your products and services, in a manner that is most beneficial to the financial standing of your business.

As part of your pricing strategy, it should be a priority to increase the perceived value of what you offer and remove any potential resistance you may encounter from your target market.

A company's pricing strategy[xvii] can have a transformative effect on its financial standing, given the influence price adjustments have on both the cash flows and the valuation of the business.

TAKE ACTION: Pricing for Profit

So how do you increase prices without getting snared by customers? By strengthening your perceived value in the market. Consider the following suggestions as a way to help you reach this goal:

- Share a story with your audience. Simple as that. You will have a better chance of succeeding with your pricing strategy if you are able to connect with your customers, their needs, and their narrative. Explain to them the value you provide through the products you offer in a way that can entertain them, or even make them happy. Telling stories is a great way to accomplish this.

- Put yourself in their shoes. Try to find out how they reason before they make a purchase decision and appeal to that reasoning. This is a far superior strategy compared to focusing on production cost and adding a margin on top of it. The benefit of doing this will be to determine whether there is room to further push prices up to a point where consumers still feel they are getting a good deal, given the value they are receiving.

- Determine how you could strategically position yourself by analyzing your competitors' pricing and positioning. Don't use price as your key differentiator in a market that prefers quality, prestige, and customer service.

- Present and package your products well. Great aesthetics create an impression of quality. More importantly, they help justify a higher price.

- Consider offering first-time discounts to attract new customers who may be skeptical or reluctant to do business with you, as an incentive or gesture of goodwill. Once their trust is earned, nurture the relationship in the hopes that they might switch later to a more valuable product.

- Give them a great deal! Everyone wants a good deal, and if you can structure your offer attractively, and at a healthy profit margin, then you have struck gold. If you use a tiered pricing model, make sure you highlight the benefits that come with each additional category to help your customer decide what they want. Consider a basic annual golf course membership for USD 10,000 for weekdays only, versus the premium annual membership for USD 15,000 inclusive of weekends and holidays. The benefits of a premium membership are that it grants weekend and holiday access and is less restrictive. As a result, it is more expensive.

- Continually test and assess how customers react and respond to changes in your pricing structure. Collect data quickly and respond accordingly.

- Improve your brand because better brands command higher prices. Take a look around you!

SMOOTH OPERATIONS

A systematic approach to your operations increases the likelihood of achieving a sustainable business with happy employees and happy customers.

An efficient operational setup[xviii] can generate significantly more output from its resources and inputs compared to its peers. Output could be defined as products and services produced, as well as volumes sold.

Core business operations are at the heart of what a business does. A chocolate manufacturer's core operations would include all activities necessary to manufacture chocolate. The core operations of an investment fund would include sourcing and executing investment opportunities, as well as monitoring investments.

Support functions, on the other hand, manage activities that support a company's core operations. For an investment fund, these may include HR, IT, finance, legal, compliance, and investor relations.

Both core and support functions are equally significant and complementary. This means that support functions cannot be ignored in favor of focusing on core functions.

When all functions in an organization are seamlessly integrated and working together, the organization stands a greater chance of achieving operational efficiency. Therefore, it will be closer to maximizing the amount of output it can generate from its inputs.

Here are a few characteristics of operationally efficient companies:

- An emphasis is placed on the customer's insights and buying journey
- Service/product quality that is consistent
- Operations and processes have been clearly defined, documented, and are understood by all
- When bottlenecks are identified, they are eliminated/resolved right away
- Employees are proficient with systems and well trained

- Key performance indicators are continuously measured, monitored, and improved

- The company honors its promises to customers and meets deadlines

TAKE ACTION: Steps to Boost Operational Efficiencies

So how does your organization become operationally efficient?

By optimizing internal processes and by enhancing the prospective customers' buying journey.

Here is a suggested framework to consider:

- Defining your business processes is the first step. That is the order in which the business acquires inputs, produces outputs, and sells them. In order to continuously improve processes, everything that happens in the back end as well as in the front end must be transparent, measurable, and methodical.

- Identify the metrics within your control that will have the greatest impact on these processes. The key to improving these metrics is in measuring them, understanding their drivers, and monitoring them.

- Make sure your core operations are supported by the right infrastructure. Ensure your organization has the right departments, is adequately staffed, and that systems that are fully utilized by trained personnel.

- Analyze your customers' buying journey. This is the process customers must navigate to complete a purchase. Ask them what they think and document their feedback so that it can be shared with other stakeholders. Make their journey hassle-free by identifying and addressing bottlenecks. Disgruntled customers can give you valuable insights into where you can improve as a company. By listening to their feedback, you may be able to prevent future customers from taking their business to a competitor.

- Do not be afraid to shake the tree. A periodic review of your workflows is often a smart idea to see if they can be improved. In most cases, the benefits of such an initiative will outweigh the burden of the task.

THE SUBTLE ART OF COMPANY CULTURE

You can make or break your strategy based on the kind of environment you create, willingly or unwillingly, within your company.

A company's culture can either be a source of pride or a source of problems. It can either be a strength or a weakness.

Moreover, it provides a valuable insight into how a company's legacy will unfold, and those influencing its direction.

An organization's culture ranges from the company's fundamental beliefs and values to the way stakeholders individually and collectively interpret and perform their roles within the organization. In other words, how they interact with each other, how they serve the market, and the meaning they attribute to their work.

The sharpest tool in your corporate toolbox is undoubtedly culture.

Companies that get their culture right[xix] tend to have the following attributes:

- They live up to their claim that their employees are their most valuable asset. They devote resources to understanding the pain points of their employees. Then they offer solutions to reduce their burdens. They believe that the more they invest in their employees and the more they instill a culture of living up to the values they claim to uphold, the better off everyone will be.

- They recognize that everyone in the organization pays close attention to the top employees, so they make sure those at the top are qualified, and that they are worthy of everyone's respect. They ensure that the organization's top team leads by example and embodies its values. They also hold everyone accountable for any breaches or misconduct, especially the top officials.

- They are fair to everyone and do not have favorite employees. In terms of setting objectives and evaluating performance, they are consistent. Through their actions, they demonstrate meritocracy over biases and favoritism.

When a company has a healthy, collaborative relationship with its employees, it has an easier time communicating performance and growth expectations. This is because it provides its employees with the right infrastructure to support their growth, to perform and exceed expectations, to collaborate, and to be invested in the success of the organization.

But sometimes, employers' actions do not reflect their claim of caring for and valuing their employees. When this happens, it shouldn't be a surprise when employees behave similarly when interacting with customers or other employees.

It's not because they are incompetent or lazy, but because they cannot escape the law of reciprocity. Their attitudes and engagement levels are directly influenced by how they perceive their employer's attitude toward them.

TAKE ACTION: Suggested Steps to Improve Company Culture

- Get to know your employees and what type of work excites them.

- Eliminate distractions when you meet with them. Make them feel heard so that they can reciprocate that same treatment with your customers.

- Ensure that employees are aware of the importance of the work they are doing and how it supports the company's strategy.

- Reinforce behaviors and actions worthy of praise by rewarding them for their efforts while adopting a less microscopic approach to their weaknesses.

- As an incentive for good work, provide flexibility and autonomy.

- Promote and reward collaboration.

- Keep employees informed regularly about important changes to the business that might impact them.

- Build an effective strategy that empowers employees and enables them to grow.

Your employees will treat each other, your customers, and your stakeholders better if they feel cared for, supported, and empowered. The culture of your company will then become a crucial asset that contributes significantly to the success and longevity of your business.

LEVERAGING TECHNOLOGY IN THE SPACE AGE

Do you like to adopt the latest technology right away or do you tend to resist it until you have no choice?

Every time a cutting-edge technology becomes available, there tends to be a buzz around it, and the buzz grows louder the more the adoption of such technologies proves valuable for business.

Today, technologies such as cloud computing, artificial intelligence, and machine learning, among others, can bring true transformations to many industries and business models due to the possibilities that they offer.

We have already seen how technology has affected operating models within brick-and-mortar retail, communication, taxis, cars, energy, conference calls, entertainment, space exploration, and many more.

And that trend is unlikely to stop, as long as technology continues to create additional pathways for value creation and improve the buying experience for customers.

Technology has and will continue to disrupt industries and change business models. It will also continue to enable companies to grow, and scale, faster than ever before.

Business Process Refresh

In order to stay relevant in their markets and industries, corporate leaders need to be aware of the changes or disruptions happening to their ecosystems.

A wise approach to change is to welcome it, to keep an open mind, and to study it closely. As obvious as it seems, it pays to be informed as early as possible rather than to arrive late.

After the change and its implications have been clearly understood, companies facing disruption can take a step back and strategize. This will enable them to identify the most critical questions that need to be addressed.

Below is a sample of such questions:

- What changes are taking place in the industry? What impact will they have on the market?

- Are we implementing a mitigation strategy? Is the risk of disruption actively and intentionally managed?

- How capable are we of adopting change and embracing the latest technology? In what ways can we use this new technology to delight our customers and retain their loyalty?

- Are we able to make use of this latest technology to enhance our product offering? Will it allow us to further optimize our internal processes?

- What resources will be required to implement such technologies?

- In what ways can we ensure we are able to implement change by our personnel and the overall organization?

As ecosystems change, customer needs change as well. You may no longer need to solve the problems that your customers once expected you to solve. Therefore, it is paramount that you continually define and assess the problems you are trying to resolve in your marketplace.

Data and People

Today's companies are proving that data, and the ability to manage large sets of it, is one of their most valuable assets. Despite it sounding like an exaggeration, there is a great deal of truth here.

Once a business figures out how to compile the right kind of data, decipher it, and use it to make informed conclusions, the data inevitably becomes a trustworthy ally.

Data is also an asset that many companies attribute a certain, in some cases very high, monetary value to. That value is often justified, especially if the data itself is proprietary, because smart companies use this data to obtain a competitive edge in the market and monetize it significantly.

Compiling high-quality data is not just a function of its source, but also a function of the people and algorithms that decipher it, interpret it, and use it to reach informed conclusions.

Additionally, it is imperative that these conclusions are communicated to decision-makers in a concise and meaningful way, so that they can truly comprehend them and use them to make the best-informed decisions possible.

An accurate set of data won't lie. It may be the most underestimated tool in your corporate toolbox.

DOMINATE INTANGIBLE ASSETS

Unlike tangible assets like real estate, machines, and equipment, assets that are deemed intangible have no physical form. Such assets include brands, patents, trademarks, designs, trade secrets, as well as operational and managerial know-how.

When considering value creation initiatives, companies may prioritize what can be seen over what cannot, so intangible assets may be placed in a lower priority bucket. This is due to the lack of outcome certainty and difficulty valuing intangible assets.

Typical reservations may sound like this:

- What are the chances that a branding investment will generate the desired return on investment?
- How long would it take for that return to materialize?
- How can a trademark improve a company's ability to service debt?
- How much money would anyone be willing to spend to acquire operational know-how? And how do we even value it?

There is no doubt that these questions are not as straightforward as quantitative and financially motivated questions. But make no mistake, intangible assets can be invaluable to shareholder value and legacy.[xx]

To further clarify, consider the following questions:

- Would you rather buy canned soup from a brand you trust than one you haven't heard of?
- Are you more likely to expect more from certain brands than others?
- Have you ever paid more for a product, such as a phone, based on your perception of the company producing it?
- In your opinion, does a brand of a fortune 500 company have any value?

- Can you think of any famous trademarks or logos of well-known companies?

- Are you able to tell the name of the company that makes your favorite product just by looking at its design?

If you've answered YES to any of the questions above, it probably means that the companies that came to your mind have done a good job with their branding strategy.

Today, consumers are more concerned than ever before about the credibility, transparency, and integrity of the companies they do business with.

Therefore, having healthy, strong, and attractive intangible assets will be a compelling reason for customers to do business with you more often.

If the market trusts your brand and what it represents, and trusts you to continuously meet expectations, staying in the game becomes easier, regardless of who runs your company.

Isn't it becoming more apparent how a company with respectable intangible assets can truly enjoy a meaningful advantage in its market?

TAKE ACTION: Maximize and Monetize Intangible Asset Value

- Evaluate your organization's intangible assets in terms of their contribution to the business. Determine the assets that have a higher contribution potential.

- Understand how your market views you. Employees who have direct contact with customers will have a good sense of customer perception. You can also gain valuable information from your data, such as the percentage of repeat customers. Customers' perceptions reveal what they trust about your company and what they expect from you. This is where you need to be objective and impartial. Then, figure out what you can do to improve that perception one step at a time.

- Make use of available media platforms and PR campaigns to pitch to the market what you are promising customers. If you truly believe you have something meaningful to offer the world, then tell the world about it. There's no other way to put it. Remember that community always brings value.

- Keep your actions in line with your words. Don't talk a big game and then disappear. Make sure your promises are backed up by the right actions, so that perception in the market is reinforced. Being consistent is equally important. You can't overdeliver in one situation and underperform in another. Invest in consistency to maintain your status. Just like a reputation, intangibles can take a long time to establish and should be well maintained.

- Contact your lawyer to determine which of your intangible assets you can register for protection against infringement.

SCALING JUST RIGHT

Are you familiar with the concept of economies of scale?

It refers to a distinct advantage that certain large firms possess over smaller ones. Since these companies produce more items, their costs, some of which are fixed and some of which are variable, are spread over a greater number of units.

As a result, they can maintain a profit margin while pricing their products at a lower price point than smaller businesses. This is due to a lower average cost per unit.

Have you ever heard of a large company pricing a smaller company out of the market? Surely you have.

So what are the steps a company needs to take to achieve scale? And is there any difference between growth and scale?

A business is scaling when its revenues are growing at a faster rate than its costs. [xxi]

This is not the same as growth. If your revenues are increasing but you are constrained by your company structure or capabilities, or if your costs are increasing at a similar rate to your revenues, you might be growing, but not scaling. In other words, you are limited by growth constraints when you aren't scaling. Among the most common growth limitations are reaching maximum operational capacity, employee constraints, resource restrictions, and time constraints.

However, if you can grow your revenues much faster than your costs, with as few constraints as possible, you're playing a different game.

When you scale, you can evolve and metamorphose quickly.

You can show momentum to secure funding, reinvest in growth, and enhance your market position.

Within a short timeframe, you can go from the small league to the big leagues.

That's the dream of every technology startup. This is how such startups can justify their sky-high valuations within a short period of time.

Their model is continuously adjusted and optimized to position themselves for scale: the state in which they can increase sales substantially while keeping cost increases minimal.

However, scaling isn't just for tech startups. It's possible for any company to find ways to improve its chances of achieving scale if it chooses to.

TAKE ACTION: Suggested Steps to Scalability

- Establish a strong infrastructure and solid foundation in order to achieve scale. Policies, procedures, processes, and systems that are clearly documented, approved by the board, and respected by all stakeholders fall into this category.

- Identify bottlenecks and issues in your business operations as soon as you can and take prompt remedial action to eliminate areas of resistance early in the scaling process.

- Explore the automation of processes and labor. Frequently, people think of automating repetitive physical labor. Today, even complex processes can be automated by leveraging machine learning and artificial intelligence. Get to know available technologies on the market that can drastically improve the efficiency of your setup. Having automated processes makes scaling much simpler.

- If you're not already doing so, set up your infrastructure to leverage proprietary data. For example, Customer Relationship Management (CRM) technology can help you leverage artificial intelligence for information gathering, sales, and marketing insights, as well as provide tailored solutions for your customers and prospects.

- Consider a digital pivot that makes sense for your company. For example, if you are in the educational space, consider developing digital education products as an added revenue stream, while focusing on the digital experience of your typical customer.

- Overcome capacity limitations through third-party partnerships. As an example, a food manufacturer that is receiving orders beyond its capacity can contract with co-packers. These are third-party food manufacturers who can produce according to specific recipes and requirements, and generally have a larger capacity to handle larger, more urgent orders.

- Establish new offices in new jurisdictions, allowing you to expand your presence and tap into new markets. Recruit experts for key positions who can generate new business and execute ideas and strategies with precision and quality.

- Explore inorganic growth through acquisitions. Taking this route can help you gain quick access to new markets, new products, and new customers. Find out more in the following pages.

INORGANIC STRATEGY

Unlike organic strategy, which relies on a company's existing capabilities and efforts, inorganic strategy seeks external capabilities to achieve strategic aims.

Mergers & Acquisitions (M&A) are executed to gain access to new markets, new products and services, new revenue streams, as well as new operational know-how and quality management teams.[xxii]

If executed successfully, M&A could provide a quicker path to growth than if a company were to earn all the same benefits on its own.

A helpful way to understand the strength of this strategy is to compare building a house from scratch with buying one that has already been built by experts and is available at a reasonable price. The acquisition route reduces execution risk, minimizes costly mistakes, and offers a quicker timeframe to get to the desired outcome.

M&A could also help complement existing forces with new ones. For example, if two similar businesses decide to merge, the combined entity could become stronger than the two entities on a standalone basis.

Consider the potential upside of combining operational know-how and client relationships, market reach, product portfolios, and relationships with banks, suppliers, and investors. Imagine selling additional products from company B to customers from company A and vice versa, benefiting from both entities' additional sales.

Advantages of Adopting an M&A Strategy

- Expanding into new markets and growing your market share will be easier and quicker.
- You will have access to new products and expertise.
- You'll be able to quickly add new revenue streams, assets, and business pipelines to your existing capabilities.

- You'll be able to share resources and achieve cost synergies and efficiencies.

- You'll be reporting bigger financial figures, which will justify a higher valuation.

- Investors and banks will be more inclined to take you seriously when your company is large.

In many ways, the process of buying or selling a company is similar to the process of buying or selling an ordinary asset, such as a home or a car. It includes finding the right opportunity, talking with the owner, negotiating a price, and closing the deal.

Company negotiations, however, are more complicated and require more time to study and analyze.

Below is a summary of the M&A process along with key milestones (we'll cover the specifics in more detail later):

- *Step 1: Deal origination (finding the right opportunity)*

- *Step 2: Initial high-level discussions between buyer and seller*

- *Step 3: Non-binding offer subject to a Due Diligence exercise (DD)*

- *Step 4: DD followed by key findings and red flag reports (with advisors, if any)*

- *Step 5: Company valuation and deal structure are finalized after DD findings are incorporated*

- *Step 6: Binding offer and signing of deal documents (such as a Sale and Purchase agreement)*

- *Step 7: Satisfaction of Conditions Precedent (CPs), if any*

- *Step 8: Deal closing and completion (exchange of funds and shares)*

Corporate development goals for blue-chip companies worldwide often include M&A. Through a quick phone call, they can access the world's best management consultants, investment banks, accounting firms, law firms, and technical advisors. They are well aware that there is substantial upside to be realized from smart deal-making, and they rarely hesitate to invest resources when attractive opportunities arise.

And they are right to consider this path. Successful deals that are executed at an attractive valuation and in appropriate conditions could help them enhance their offering and positioning in their key markets. Additionally, they could help them realize significant synergies, gains, efficiencies, and growth.

For a publicly listed company, a quality acquisition with decent growth prospects may be well received by the market, leading to a rise in the company's stock price.

Rather than taking the long way to success, why not use a shortcut that is often explored and used by world-leading companies?

In the following section, we'll cover inorganic strategy in more detail, suggesting steps you can take today to assess how exploring this path might serve your interests.

Checklist: Exploring Growth Through M&A

- What are my strategic objectives for the company? Can those aspirations be realized with existing resources and capabilities? If so, how long will it take?

- If money and resources weren't a factor, what could help my firm become more valuable? What can I do to develop these capabilities sooner? Could I integrate such capabilities into my business if I acquired them externally rather than developing them myself?

- Could there be an acquisition target on the market that matches that profile?

- What is my level of confidence in my ability to close a deal? During due diligence, what would I look for? Do I need advisors? How would I choose them?

- How will I leverage my existing capabilities to maximize the value from the acquired assets?

The Buyer Questionnaire

Imagine you are the owner of a food production business. A competitor of yours, whom you respect and admire, is considering selling their business.

You are interested in pursuing the opportunity as a potential buyer, and so you reach out and set up a meeting with the owner.

You intend to demonstrate that you are serious, and so, for the purpose of the first meeting, you want to come up with a list of questions that helps you build rapport with the seller.

Here's a suggested list of questions for doing just that:

- How did you get started with your business? How did you end up where you are today? How would you describe current the state of your business?

- What are your thoughts on the market? What do you think about the industry and the competition?

- If you could go back in time, what would you have done differently?

- What are the biggest challenges you are facing in the business today? If you could make the top three problems in the business disappear, which ones would you choose?

- What are some of your high-level revenue and profit numbers over the last three years? Has the business been growing? How much debt is currently sitting on the business? How much free cash flow does the business generate per annum?

- Are your employees aware of your plans to sell? What does your current management team look like? How long have they been with the company?

- What are the reasons behind your decision to sell the business now? Have you been trying to sell the business for a long time? Are you in discussions with other buyers?

- How does your shareholding structure look? Are you the only owner? If not, how are things with your fellow shareholders? Would they be interested in selling as well?

- What does an ideal buyer look like to you? What are the things you hope the incoming buyer will do for the business?

- Is there a timeline you have in mind for the sale?

These questions serve you in more ways than just collecting data points on the business.

By discussing the history of the company and the owner's journey, you will build a stronger connection with the seller and develop the necessary rapport with them.

You will get an indication of the numbers and a rough estimate of where the valuation could be once the books are open.

These questions also focus on the motives, intentions, and pain points of the seller.

During the discussion, neither side should develop a negative attitude, or feel as if they are walking on eggshells.

Both parties should honestly evaluate whether to pursue these discussions further and invest resources in the process following the initial meeting.

Also, a careful decision must be made during the preliminary discussions about whether valuation should be discussed. It may be premature to bring up this topic if you don't have a good understanding of how the business works.

If you give the seller a figure that is too low, they may not be willing to continue discussions.

On the other hand, if at first you give a high number but then open the books and see that the numbers don't add up, the negotiations could get messy.

Selling Moves

Now let's sit on the other side of the table in a different hypothetical scenario.

Imagine you are a business owner who is looking to sell a partial or full stake in the business. And you have absolutely no clue where to start or what to do.

Before you do anything, you need to plan the sale process itself. You need to strategize on how to make the sale process easy for the incoming buyer, starting with preliminary discussions which will include an overview of the opportunity.

You will need to have a story that highlights the merits of the business and its potential.

There will be a number of things you will want to demonstrate. These include how well the company has performed, if there are other shareholders involved and, of course, the genuine reason you wish to sell.

The next few pages will provide a template for doing that, along with a few examples.

Business Seller – Opportunity Overview Template

- Business Overview: What does the company do? How does it benefit the market? Think about how you would briefly explain your business to someone you just met at a trade show. Include key operational metrics such as number of employees, capacity, and utilization.

- Financial Overview: How has the business been performing? Is it growing? Include key financial metrics such as revenues, operating profit, net income, and net debt.

- Ownership Structure: What is the ownership structure of the business? Are you the sole proprietor? Does the company have other shareholders? If so, are they all interested in selling?

- Deal Overview: What kind of deal structure are you looking for? What percentage of your business are you selling? If you are selling a partial stake, will the proceeds be reinvested into the company? If applicable, how will the funds invested into the business be allocated?

Let's look at a few examples.

- **PRIME FALSE CEILINGS LLC**
  - Business Overview: The Chicago suburbs-based Prime False Ceilings LLC (PFC) provides bespoke false ceiling services to residential and commercial clients. Services include design, installation, and after-service. The company employs 50 people and is currently operating at full capacity. There are currently ten projects on the waiting list for this year.

  - Financial Overview: Over the last three years, revenues have grown by an average of 6%. The business generated USD 12 million in revenue last year and earned USD 2.5 million in profit. The business recently upgraded its systems, and its cash position is about USD 300,000. In any given month, the maximum cash requirement for the business is USD 200,000, so there's about USD 100,000 in excess cash.

  - Ownership Structure: Ownership of the company is divided between two equal partners who are actively involved in the day-to-day activities of the business and one passive partner who is not involved. Each active owner owns 40% of the company and receives a salary of USD 95,000. The passive owner owns the remaining 20% and is entitled to a pro rata share of dividends paid.

- Proposed Deal Structure and Timeline: Each of the two active shareholders is selling a 20% stake in the company. Consequently, a 40% stake in the company is being offered for sale. After having doubled the business over the past five years, the two active shareholders want to monetize some of the value they created. Following the transaction, they each plan to retain a 20% ownership stake and remain actively involved in the business. They plan to close the deal within the next six months. Their shortlist of potential investors is determined based on a combination of price, investor relevance, as well as value-add. They prefer investors with experience in the industry.

This may seem like too much information at first, but it makes a world of difference to someone hearing about the opportunity for the first time. Know-how and transparency are exhibited, as well as generosity in the exchange of information. Providing generous information gives the impression you are transparent and are looking to build rapport with the people with whom you will have business discussions. Furthermore, you'll alleviate any skepticism or resistance they might have toward the opportunity by showing that you've already considered their possible questions.

- **ELI HEALTH**
  - Business Overview: Elizabeth is the 65-year-old founder and owner of Eli Health, a holistic healing training institute in downtown Los Angeles. She is seeking to retire and is considering selling her business. The institute has been operational for 15 years and enjoys a strong brand in the market. It provides in-person training and has a capacity of 200 trainees per module. A training module costs on average

USD 4,000 per student, lasts about six weeks, and leads to an accredited certification. Over the last three years, Eli Health offered six modules per year on average, at full capacity. Even though Elizabeth comes into the office once a week, she is not involved in the day-to-day operations.

○ Financial Overview: In the last year, revenues were USD 4,800,000, operating profit was USD 2,500,000, and net income was USD 1,500,000. The company has no debt on its books. Cash is collected upfront, before a module begins, and the business has been consistently profitable over the last 10 years.

○ Ownership structure: Elizabeth is the sole owner of the business and owns 100% of the shares outstanding.

○ Proposed Deal Structure and Timeline: Elizabeth wishes to sell the entire business and is willing to help with the transition for a maximum of three months. Despite her willingness to facilitate a handover period for up to three months, she believes the existing management team can handle the transition, and therefore, her presence is not necessary. Her reason for selling is that she feels she has taken the business as far as it can go. She now intends to retire in Massachusetts so she can live near her daughters and grandchildren.

Based on the above, a prospective buyer could infer the following:

• The star founder is looking for a full exit, so it is imperative that her departure won't create risk or negatively impact day-to-day operations.

• Given Eli Health is a well-known brand in the market it serves, the new owner needs to consider whether it is worthwhile to keep or change the name after Elizabeth leaves.

- The training institute appears to be financially healthy, pending confirmation of due diligence findings.

- With a strong desire to retire, Elizabeth seems to be a motivated seller. Her goal is to complete the sale smoothly and on time. She would not want the deal to take too long to close.

- **TRUE INSIGHTS**

  - Business Overview: True Insights is a survey and market research company based in New Haven, Connecticut. In order to assist clients in making informed marketing decisions, the firm conducts quantitative and qualitative research. The company is headed by its founder and owner, Tim, and employs 35 people.

  - Financial Overview: Last year, the business generated USD 10,200,000 in sales with a net profit of USD 3,500,000. In the past three years, revenue has grown by an average of 7% per annum. The business does not have any debt.

  - Ownership Structure: Tim has owned and led the business since it was established 20 years ago.

  - Proposed Deal Structure: Tim wants to raise USD 3,000,000 in exchange for a 25% stake in the business. The deal proceeds will be used to establish a new office in Boston so that the company can provide on-the-ground support to Boston-based clients, who contribute about 50% to total sales. Melanie, Tim's daughter, who currently leads business development, will relocate to the Boston office full time. She will also be leading the team's recruitment efforts. The opportunity is to own a stake in the entire company and not just the upcoming Boston office.

The key takeaway here is that the owner is seeking growth capital and collaboration via a partnership, rather than a complete exit. As Tim is looking to set up a new office, he is looking for a new partner to join him. Tim believes that the Boston-expansion opportunity has merit and is financially viable. Additionally, he is planning to remain with the company and continue leading it.

Here is what the profile of an ideal investor might look like:

- Strong knowledge of the market and the industry
- Seeking to partner with a capable management team
- Is not interested in being actively involved in the business
- A willingness to facilitate opportunities for business development within their network

Keeping Promises

In this section, we will discuss how seemingly innocent, yet very common, statements made by eager sellers at the beginning of the sales process can backfire and harm the deal.

It would be frustrating for a seller to spend three months compiling information for an interested investor, only to discover they were unknowingly misrepresenting information, and that the business dynamics weren't aligned with what they had initially claimed.

Transparency and honesty about the product being sold, which in this case is an entire business, will minimize the risk of bad faith bargaining and a failed sale.

Regardless of how silly the questions may seem, it is wise for sellers to acknowledge any doubts that they may have regarding such questions.

In the end, everyone evaluates opportunities according to their own criteria, so a seller is always better off answering "I'm not completely sure I have an answer to that question at this time" than responding incorrectly to questions a prospective investor is taking note of.

Examples of Misrepresentations by Sellers

- *Hypothesis*: *"We do not have any cash flow issues. The business is self-funded, and our pipeline is very promising."*

  Reality: This is a hypothesis that would instantly resonate with an investor. If it is true, it is clearly a great thing. If it isn't, a review of the bank statements and audited financial statements would invalidate this hypothesis.

- *Hypothesis:* *"We don't have issues with the collection of outstanding receivables. We enjoy a robust relationship with our clients and go directly to the decision-maker when any payment issue arises."*

  Reality: The notes to the financial statements usually include a schedule showing the aging of receivables. Otherwise, an accounting due diligence exercise will show the current state of outstanding receivables. Overdue receivables could indicate cash flow problems for the company, especially if they constitute a significant percentage of the revenues booked by the business.

- *Hypothesis:* *"We are extremely busy and stretched. We are looking to hire more people."*

  Reality: An investor will have reservations about the entire business model and its resilience if a due-diligence review shows that the company has cash-flow issues, despite claims of being busy. In the event that a seller claims they are overstretched, they need to be prepared to show good operational and financial figures that would get a buyer excited. Otherwise, a business might lose its appeal due to its limited ability to withstand a market slowdown or tougher competition, in which case cash flows would decline, causing difficulties.

- *Hypothesis: "We don't need to incur any capital expenditure (Capex) over the next five years."*

Reality: The audited statements, the fixed asset register, or a simple inspection by a technical consultant can reveal the age and useful life of fixed assets. If a seller shows essential assets to be in poor shape (e.g., a chocolate manufacturing machine for a chocolate manufacturer), it is likely that the incoming buyers, or the business, will have to invest in updated equipment over the next few years. This will entail a cash outflow which might come at the expense of dividends that the investor would want to sweep from the business, or other expenses required for the business to operate. And if that capital expenditure is not incurred, imagine what's going to happen to the business once its equipment is fully worn out. Would you acquire a chocolate manufacturing company for full price, if you knew that its main asset is dysfunctional and will need to be repaired or replaced at some point in the future? How will the operations of your business and your investment be affected if your main asset fails?

- *Hypothesis: "If managed properly, the business will generate a 15% return on investment."*

Reality: That's a very big "if." It looks like a lot of risk and work for an investor to take on, because if the key person in the business can't manage it properly, the investor could face even more difficulties. In addition, if a seller shows low margins and claims someone else will have higher margins because they will manage the business better, then, quite frankly, that's not value the seller is entitled to be paid for. Consider selling a house in poor condition and saying, "If fixed, this house could be worth an extra USD 400,000, so I will ask for an extra USD 400,000."

- *Hypothesis: "The team is phenomenal and requires almost no input from me. The business can run without my presence and is almost entirely automated."*

  Reality: This statement will be put to the test through the due diligence exercise, which will allow an incoming investor to ascertain the strength, attitude, and character of those in criterial roles as well as the organizational structure of the company. If, for example, the owner is the only person who has direct access to clients or the company's bank accounts, then that hypothesis could be disproved.

- *Hypothesis: "I am asking for a high valuation because this business has so much potential, which makes it a fantastic investment opportunity."*

  Reality: Why has the existing seller not taken advantage of that potential to begin with? In what way does the seller claim they need to be compensated for that potential, knowing they weren't able to unlock it themselves? Furthermore, why would an incoming investor pay upfront for potential that they, or the people they would bring in, need to work hard to monetize? We all overvalue potential. The savvy seller uses it to their advantage, and the savvy investor doesn't fall for it.

- *Hypothesis: "I've invested a lot of money in my business, so I think I'm asking for a fair price."*

  Reality: If a seller asks for a higher price than the business is worth, they are likely to be met with resistance from a buyer. In the end, what matters is the intrinsic value of the business at the time of sale, not the price that makes the seller happy and excited. These two prices are very different. When comparable businesses are being sold for a multiple of 6x earnings, and the seller requests a multiple of 12x earnings, it is unlikely that the seller will succeed in selling their business.

The Moment of Truth

Due Diligence (DD) refers to the study a prospective investor conducts, along with their advisor(s), when assessing an investment opportunity.

In some ways, most people conduct DD without calling it that. As an example, you might consider buying a used car from a dealer and request to test drive it first. Perhaps you would like to make an offer on a house that is on the market and would like a real estate professional to take a look at it. In both cases, you are making a decision based on certain information about the asset you are looking to purchase. More importantly, you are looking to determine whether the price you are expected to pay is justified. If it isn't, you may counteroffer or walk away.

The DD exercise is expected to achieve the following aims:

- To test, challenge, or verify the investment thesis around the contemplated opportunity.

- To assess potential risks, or red flags, associated with the acquisition target.

- To determine whether the initial valuation discussed between the buyer and seller holds up after conducting a deep dive into the specifics of the business.

In the event that the DD exercise reveals red flags that no longer justify the initial valuation, the buyer could, in some cases, walk away from the deal or submit a revised valuation to the seller.

A downward adjustment to the valuation is not the best news to share with any seller, especially after they have opened all their books for you, gathered all the data you've requested, answered all your questions, and facilitated meetings with their management team. Therefore, it is advisable to explain to them why the valuation was adjusted downward, especially given they are already anchored to the initial valuation which was agreed to in the non-binding agreement.

If the seller is still keen to pursue the deal, then both parties can move to negotiate and sign the legally binding contract at a lower price than the one originally agreed to in the non-binding agreement. As a reminder, the non-binding agreement is executed by both parties prior to the DD exercise.

In the scenario above, the DD exercise turned out to be eye opening and helped the prospective investor realize that the initial valuation did not hold, thereby saving them the entire amount of the adjustment to the valuation. Many investors resist the idea of conducting DD thoroughly, primarily due to time or resource constraints. Wiser investors never compromise on the DD process, regardless of how long it takes or how much it costs.

DD is usually a time-bound process. Prior to the start of the exercise, it is given a deadline.

Additionally, prospective investors, along with their advisors, need to compile and send an Information Request List (IRL) to the sellers and their advisors, if applicable. This may be followed by one or multiple face-to-face management meetings, to make sure that all the requested data has been delivered, and that no further clarifications are needed.[xxiii]

Due Diligence Streams

The following are common due diligence streams a prospective investor may follow to prove or disprove their investment thesis regarding an acquisition opportunity.

Financial Due Diligence

An assessment of the business's financial health. This involves conducting a deep dive into the historical financial statements and accounts of the business. Among the items to evaluate are the quality of earnings, normalized EBITDA, working capital, debt, cash, taxes, and fixed assets.

Legal Due Diligence

A detailed study to identify legal red flags and avoid potential future litigation for the incoming investor. It would be considered a red flag if the business is involved in a legal dispute with a supplier over payment delays. Potential losses arising from the lawsuit may be incurred by the incoming owner. All legal documents necessary for the sale could also be prepared, reviewed, and edited by legal advisors. For example, the sale and purchase agreement (SPA) is a key document for closing the deal that is usually prepared, edited, and negotiated by lawyers from both parties.

Commercial Due Diligence

As a typical example, this would include an expert's perspective on the market and the target company's competitive position, along with a custom scope of work, which may include, but is not limited to:

- An audit of the operations of the business
- A thorough review and build-up of a forward-looking business plan
- Suggestions for various initiatives to derive more value from the business going forward

Technical Due Diligence

This refers to getting an opinion from technical experts specific to an industry or business model.[xxiv] Consider a medical center that has extensive biomedical equipment as an example. A biomedical engineering review would assess the quality and value of the hospital's equipment. An assessment of the equipment's condition, whether it's been maintained properly, and whether any items should be replaced, as well as the cost of maintenance and replacements would be part of the scope of work. Experts could also advise on any additional equipment needed to expand the service offering of the center.

Real Estate Due Diligence

Any real estate that is owned by the business, related to the deal, should be evaluated by an expert for its market value and condition.

Real-Life Examples of DD Red Flags

Here are some real-life examples that illustrate the types of red flags that can appear at the end of a due diligence process. There may not be two businesses that are exactly alike, but there are frequently common themes or patterns that can be observed through due diligence:

- Among 15 sales employees, two generate over 90% of sales. Each is paid the same, fixed salary.

- All approvals are given by the founder, who has absolute authority over all aspects of the business. Currently, there are no qualified candidates for leadership roles in the organization. In the event that the business is sold and the founder leaves, a new leader must be recruited externally.

- There are no warranties provided by the seller. Meaning after the deal is concluded, there will be no recourse to the exiting seller whatsoever.

- Due to a defect in their last project, the company is currently under litigation with a long-standing client. The client suffered material losses and is suing the seller for USD 3,000,000. The lawsuit comes at a time when the company's license is due for renewal.

- In a few months, the lease for the office building will be renewed with a 35% increase, which will adversely affect the company's profits.

- As new competitors enter the market, the business is currently facing downward pricing pressure.

- Two checks to suppliers bounced in the past two months, totaling USD 1,200,000.

- It is estimated that USD 2,100,000 will be needed to improve the electrical, mechanical, and plumbing systems in the business's building.

- Over 50% of the outstanding receivables have been overdue for more than two years.

- Even though the business reported a profit last year, its free cash flow was zero. This is due to working capital issues that put a strain on its cash flow.

- Maintenance contracts are expired, and the equipment is fully depreciated. The business must invest in new equipment, which will have to be funded externally because it does not have enough cash to make such an investment on its own.

- Approximately 40% of junior employees resigned in the last three years. They served an average of four months before they resigned. Their resignations were not justified or validated. Finding a replacement took an average of two months. Also, there is no HR department in the company, and hiring is outsourced to a recruitment firm.

- The business relies on no software to streamline its operations. There is also resistance to embracing technology, and a preference for pen and paper is evident. The staff is overburdened with mundane administrative tasks.

- The firm is audited by a company that is owned by the brother-in-law of the largest shareholder.

- While the due diligence period was ongoing, the seller refused to let the incoming buyers speak to the employees, arguing that they did not want them worrying about their future and disrupting operations. Consequently, it was not possible to assess the quality of the employees, the challenges they face, or their opinion of the company's culture.

- The seller seems reluctant to share information during the due diligence process, as many of the requested items remain unanswered.

- The seller is pushing to close the deal even though many of the requested information is still pending.

- Despite the seller's claim that the company has just been put up for sale, a broker that the investor knows has confirmed that it has been on the market for two years.

M&A Jargon Is Just Jargon

Here is a list of the most common terms seen in the M&A space and what they mean.

Mergers & Acquisitions

An acquisition is when one company takes ownership over, or "absorbs", another company, whereas a merger is the coming together of two companies to form a new legal entity.

Non-binding Agreement

A preliminary legal agreement, usually referred to as a Letter of Intent (LOI), Memorandum of Understanding (MoU), or Heads of Terms (HoT), that is executed in good faith between the seller and the buyer. Agreements of this type lay out expectations early in the deal process, and are followed by a due diligence exercise, which would involve detailed information gathering and analysis by the buyer, and their advisors if applicable. From that point on, they can solidify their understanding of the business and ensure they haven't missed out on key findings in their assessment. Parties can still back out from a deal after signing a non-binding agreement. However, such an agreement indicates both parties are serious about exploring the deal, as the DD stage entails an investment of time and resources by both parties to complete.

Binding Agreement

A legal agreement that binds both parties, the buyer and the seller, so that they can no longer back out of the deal. In an M&A transaction, an example of a binding agreement is the Sale and Purchase agreement (SPA), which is signed after the due diligence exercise is complete to the satisfaction of the buyer, and the valuation is agreed to the satisfaction of both parties.

Representations and Warranties

A deal's success is predicated on the exchange of accurate information and the provision of warranties during the deal negotiation process. Representations are the facts or information a party shares and the warranties assure that the information shared is accurate and true, with an implied promise. When there is a breach by either a seller or a buyer, the affected party is entitled to be compensated for the harm or loss incurred (indemnification). Representations and warranties are generally included in binding agreements.

Common warranties sought by buyers:

- The audited accounts state correct information about the company's profits, assets, and liabilities.

- The company is not in default under any contract executed.

- The list of employees and their remuneration is accurate.

- There are no circumstances that are likely to give rise to any litigation proceedings against the company.

Indemnities

An indemnity is a security (a promise to reimburse) against "broken promises or statements" in the transaction agreement. Think of indemnities as specific, quantifiable compensation for specific events.

The buyer, for example, will seek indemnification (dollar for dollar) from the seller for actions taken by management during the deal process that are outside of the ordinary course of business and in violation of the terms of the agreement. This is because such actions may negatively impact the incoming shareholder's financial standing once they receive the shares and take ownership of the target company.

Reserved Matters

Reserved matters refer to pre-defined actions that are excluded from a binding agreement because they require special approvals if they arise.

A passive investor with a minority stake in a company might not have any say in the day-to-day operations but might require a say over certain actions that are deemed to materially affect their investment. As part of the reserved matters, they would define the actions requiring, for example, the unanimous consent of all the shareholders.

Examples of reserved matters, in this case, would include:

- Altering the memorandum of association of the company
- Acquiring or merging with another business
- Paying bonuses to key staff
- Initiating litigation against any counterparty
- Liquidating company assets

The more extensive the reserved matters, the more complex the negotiations can be.

Conditions Precedent

A legally binding contract signed by both parties may include certain conditions, the Conditions Precedent (CPs), that must be fulfilled before it becomes effective.

Examples of CPs include:

- Obtaining necessary approvals from regulatory bodies
- Obtaining necessary approvals from all shareholders
- Obtaining necessary approvals from banks
- Agreeing on a settlement with departing managers or staff

These conditions or events are typically included in the SPA and must be agreed to by both buyer and seller.

Deal Completion

As soon as the CPs are satisfied, the funds and shares can be exchanged, and the deal is considered closed.

CONCLUDING ORGANIC AND INORGANIC CORPORATE STRATEGY

And that's a wrap for our strategy section!

Throughout this section, we covered the different ways leadership teams can cultivate and grow their business, both organically and inorganically.

According to business research, only a minority of business leaders excel at both strategy and execution. Therefore, a promising strategy will always fall short if there is no buy-in from those who matter: those who allocate resources and those who are driven to execute.

The good thing is that strategy tends to be a popular and exciting discussion topic across companies, especially because successful outcomes reflect positively on everyone involved.

Most people enjoy talking strategy. Fewer people enjoy executing a strategy. The successful ones are those that do both.

Next Steps: Corporate Strategies You Can Start Adopting Today

Here are a few suggestions that will help your business achieve more prosperity through effective strategy:

- Define your strategic intent by assessing your current situation, your resources, and your long-term goals.

- Your budget and your business plan should be ambitious yet attainable, and something that both you and your team support and believe in.

- Measure and monitor KPIs across your operations for optimal improvements and efficiency. As the saying goes, everything that can be measured can be improved.

- Take advantage of your existing products and services to innovate before your competition does. Also, assess the merits of launching new products and entering new markets.

- Assess your ability to raise prices for popular products that have a differentiated positioning in the market. Identify products that are not selling, and redirect your resources and efforts to other, more popular products. Make sure you are within your perceived value range on your price. Also, make sure your gross profit margins are sufficient to cover your needs and support your business plan forecasts.

- Evaluate your technology competency. If you are anti-tech, get someone else to do the research on your behalf. Avoid being intimidated by technological disruption, or you run the risk of adopting a passive strategy, leaving yourself and the business behind.

- Be intentional about your brand, your culture, and your intangible assets so they can serve you while you sleep.

- Consider expanding by acquiring, merging, or forming joint ventures with other businesses.

- Develop a shortlist of potential targets for acquisitions, joint ventures, public/private partnerships, and strategic investments.

- Establish strategic partnerships and mutual referrals that can funnel more business your way and provide new revenue streams.

MAGICAL CHARISMA

Leadership is an action, not a position

—Donald McGannon

We will discuss exemplary leadership as the final enabler on our corporate value creation journey. This is probably the most important enabler of all, as it unites and maximizes the effects of all the other enablers.

It is a game-changer when a business has inspiring role models that people respect and choose to follow, no matter what challenges are thrown at them.

In this chapter, we will be looking at key leadership qualities that enable value creation, and more importantly, leave organizations and those serving them better off.

This section will analyze the qualities of those who spent years influencing and taking chances on others. People who are admired by their followers not because of short-term self-interest, but rather because of who they are personally, the causes they represent, and the lasting impact they've made.[xxv]

There is no shortage of interpretations of what constitutes outstanding leadership. And although entirely subjective, my favorite interpretation of outstanding leaders is: Those who take others on journeys they never imagined possible.

Unlike the popular belief that leaders are born, not made, I believe there is a method to bring out great leadership in others. And with awareness comes everything. Therefore, we will not only focus on key leadership traits in this chapter, but also discuss some limitations that we all have, like irrational biases, limiting beliefs, and a resistance to change. We will then argue that there is a significant probability that, if we choose to, we can still manifest every ounce of leadership potential we still possess.

Think of this chapter as a reminder of something important that you already know, and an agitator to put your leadership, and the leadership of those you believe in, on the radar again.

Looking at The Stars

> *"We are all in the gutter, but some of us are looking at the stars."*
>
> —Oscar Wilde

Exemplary leadership is about providing guidance and direction that influence the company's overall success. Good leaders are known for being persuasive, empathetic, and visionary. They are intimate with their strengths and are aware of their limitations. They lead by example and bring out the best in others. More importantly, they know that true leadership is about serving others.

15 Traits of Exemplary Leaders

1. Empathy

You are more likely to influence others when you can demonstrate an accurate understanding of their position.

That understanding can be demonstrated in a variety of ways:

- Recognizing, understanding, and acknowledging another person's thoughts

- Feeling an emotion that another person feels: I'm happy when I see that you are happy

- Movement that mirrors movement: your neighbor smiles at you in the morning on the way to work, and you smile back

- Feeling a physical sensation that another person feels: it pains me to see you in pain

Empathy training is encouraged by institutions at the highest levels, and companies set aside substantial budgets for such development. Corporations know that empathy and leadership are directly correlated, and that having better leaders means a stronger impact in the market and a better bottom line.

Even the science shows that parts of our brain light up when we consciously observe someone doing something, almost as though we are doing it ourselves. This is empathy, and we are wired for it.

So, why not nurture this trait that is already wired into our brains?

2. Conscientiousness

Before they go on to lead others, those who are conscientious are experts at leading themselves. They have evolved to control their impulses; they are organized and diligent in their work with a strong eye for detail. They've developed the resilience needed to stay in their chosen game and persevere in the face of adversity. They are reliable and are not afraid to hold themselves accountable. They roll their sleeves up and act like coaches when they need to. Who would you consider to be conscientious in your circle of influence?

3. Integrity

Their actions match their promises, and they lead by example. They are not driven by their own personal gains and agendas, but by the wellbeing of the ecosystem they are leading, and the causes they value most. They are genuine and authentic, and your gut instincts around them make you feel that they are someone you can trust and respect.

4. Rapport Building

Rapport is the ability to build an emotional connection with others which, if done properly, sets the stage for trust and cooperation. It is about creating "chemistry" with others, even if it is not felt initially. The first step in building rapport is being genuinely curious about what people want to share with you, so that their sense of self-identity is tied into your conversations. Active listening is a great way of demonstrating such curiosity. Always aim to build rapport. The benefits of having good rapport include having more flexibility and less resistance around crucial matters in high stake conversations.

5. Reciprocity

Instead of upholding the narrative of "if you give me, I will give you," why not give first? Why not take the first step in giving, in hopes that the party on the receiving end will play by the code and give back? It is a paradox. To get more of something, you must give more of that same thing. If you smile at someone, chances are they will smile back at you. If you invite someone to your house, you are more likely to be invited to theirs. Similarly, if you come across as trusting and respectful to people, they are more likely to reciprocate that trust and respect.

6. Sense of Humor

Have you ever heard the saying: "a sense of humor is the best business card"? Studies continue to show that people who exhibit a good sense of humor are more likable. Having a good sense of humor is a sign of psychological maturity because it enables you to step out of your one-sided perspective and recognize and acknowledge tough situations. It also helps disarm the counterparty and encourage others to share more with you.

7. Excellent Communicators

Those who are skilled at saying the right things at the right time and in the right manner, are more likely to have effective conversations. They would rather stay in silence than say something that would detract from the progress on an important topic. They are good at listening and know how to ask the right questions. They are also good at picking up on what is left unsaid, on body language, and on facial expressions. Even on the tones and vocal variety used. Being an excellent communicator is about having a presence so that when you speak, people listen and remember what you said in the way you intended.

8. Persuasive

Persuasion is accomplished by influencing someone's thoughts, attitudes, or behavior without coming across as assertive.

Here are a few things that help make you more persuasive:

- Have social proof: You are more likely to buy a product online when you see 100 positive reviews from total strangers who have purchased, tried, and tested it. Similarly, you are more likely to laugh at a boring joke if everyone around you is laughing hysterically.

- Appeal to the other party's rules and values: The more you invest in getting to know others, the more insight you get into their priorities, values, and stated positions. To be able to persuade, you need to agitate the other side's personal or collective narrative.

- Appeal to reason: Reason is a universal language that has a high chance of resonating with others. Combined with emotional and psychological aspects, appealing to reason strengthens your appeal and makes you more persuasive.

9. Fantastic Negotiators

The best negotiations tend to be those that are approached as a win-win, collaborative effort where the deal itself, not the counterparty, is the adversary. Those who negotiate with good negotiators complete a deal feeling heard and respected. They trust that what comes next is in line with what was communicated and agreed upon. They carry on their lives without feeling deceived or exploited at any point throughout the process.

10. Great storytellers

Stories form connections. They captivate the listener's attention, energy, emotions, personal narrative, and imagination. Stories are far more memorable than slides, brochures, lists, and mountains of information. They also make the narrator more memorable and more likable.

Questions to consider when delivering an impactful story:

- Who is my core audience?

- How can I narrate my story in a manner that my audience can relate to?

- What can I add to the story from my own life experiences that would make what I'm saying more relatable? Perhaps acknowledge difficulties and struggles I've had?

- What is the cause I am inviting my audience to be part of?

11. They Embrace Taking and Giving Feedback

Constructive feedback is more likely to be adopted if the recipient feels agitated enough to act but not judged and/or coerced into making behavioral changes. Great leaders know how to do just that. And sometimes, feedback is most effective when communicated informally, rather than through formal feedback sessions.

12. Inquisitive Yet Non-Judgmental

Leaders with this trait have mastered the ability to ask the right questions in the right manner. They ensure the delivery of their questions is non-judgmental, which helps people lower their guard and volunteer information more comfortably. They are interested in resolving problems and moving forward, without dwelling on who to blame.

Examples of calibrated questions:

- How do you usually make decisions that are critical to the interests of the organization? How often do you reflect on the decision-making process?

- What are the outcomes you were seeking when you made this decision?

- On a scale of 1 to 10, how executable do you think that idea is? What do we need to plan and do today in order to get one step ahead on that scale?

- What's going to happen if we take this step?

- How has this strategy served you in the past?

- If you could go back in time, knowing what you know now, what would you do differently regarding X?

- Is this something you think the organization can never achieve? What makes you think that?

- How did this problem come about? How did this all start? How did we reach the situation we have here? How do we overcome the challenge we have here?

13. Discipline

Those who become great at leading others are great at leading themselves. This means they are disciplined and organized in how they approach complex tasks. Once a task is deemed a priority, they do what needs to be done: making a difficult call, putting their personal interests on standby, and taking all the necessary steps to get the momentum going on the task at hand, irrespective of whether they enjoy doing that task or not.

There is pain in discipline. It requires structure and commitment. There is also power in discipline. It offers a sense of purpose, clarity, and drive to continue achieving. It also makes you more in tune with your leadership capabilities.

14. Creators of Opportunities

Their mindset is one of creating opportunities, and they don't consider life a zero-sum game.

In an age where many of us tend to seek instant gratification and pursue our own selfish interests, they come across as "givers."

When discussing opportunities or change with others, they come prepared to the conversation and already know the answer to the famous question: "What's in it for me?"

15. Unashamed to Change their Mind

It is a leader's job to make informed decisions that consider accurate, current, and reliable data. It is also a leader's responsibility to reevaluate that decision when new conflicting data comes into the equation and compromises the strength of the original hypothesis.

They understand that no decision should be a death sentence, and no path should be fatal. They know and act like they always have a choice. And the truth is, we all do.

Passing the Torch

As the saying goes, it takes one to know one.

Great leaders can spot leadership traits and great qualities in others, regardless of their seniority. They are good at attracting competent people who are looking for the right environment to channel their contributions.

They realize that the potential for growth of an organization is directly related to its human potential. It is clear to them that with the right leadership to carry on the legacy, the future of the organization is just as promising, if not more so, than ever before.

They also realize that their legacy will reflect the kind of leadership they left behind after their departure.

Do you have a solid foundation for your legacy in place?

- Have you decided what kind of leadership you will need to implement succession planning?

- Have you identified potential leaders within the organization?

- Have you started exploring ways to develop those potential leaders and equip them with the skills they are going to need?

- Have you had discussions with them about their future with the business?

RATIONALIZING THE IRRATIONAL

Not every decision we make is entirely pragmatic.

That's because human nature is, to a large extent, irrational.

In business and in life, we fall for many irrational biases that could harm our progress.[xxvi]

Being aware of such biases and being able to identify them and label them gives us a powerful advantage.

WE ARE IRRATIONAL BEINGS

Loss Aversion

Everyone has a loss aversion, and so this bias is probably hardwired into everyone's brain.

Due to loss aversion, we feel much worse about losing something than we feel good about gaining something of equal value.

Confirmation Bias

The tendency to search for, interpret, favor, and recall information in a way that confirms our views and beliefs rather than yield to objective thinking. This can lead businesses to underestimate their weaknesses and risks and overestimate their strengths and capabilities.

Anchor Bias

This bias refers to the tendency to rely too heavily on the first piece of information during the decision-making process. This is prevalent in business negotiations, particularly in relation to pricing. The anchor thrown (e.g., the deal value) often sets the tone for the entire negotiation, and any material deviations from the anchored price will be met with resistance from the seller.

Overconfidence Bias

A tendency to overestimate one's abilities and ideas diminishes the ability to accept corrective evidence when it exists.

This makes it more difficult to persuade, influence, or negotiate effectively when others have compelling reasons to disagree with us.

Herding Bias

This refers to our instinctive tendency to follow the crowd.

Whether we like to admit it or not, we are social creatures, constantly looking for validation from our peers.

An example of herding can be seen in the stock market, where many of us take cues from unqualified friends, rather than conducting our independent research, speaking with a professional, or deciding on an exposure that best suits our ability and willingness to take certain risks.

Disorder of Power

This is when people who have had prolonged exposure to power become unwilling and unable to accept criticism or correctly interpret events that diverge from their beliefs. In business and politics, this bias cannot be overstated.

Sunk Cost Fallacy

This is when we continue to hold onto something or take a predetermined course of action because it seems impossible to lose after our sacrifices have been made. If I have dedicated multiple years of my life to a venture that is objectively failing, I am probably going to resist moving on, because I feel like I need to have something to show for my sacrifices.

It can be tricky, and difficult, because sometimes it is a better decision to cut our losses and move on.

Overvaluing Potential

The tendency to oversimplify what is unknown, underestimate how long things take, and overestimate what is achievable.

Limiting Beliefs

Our limiting beliefs keep us from feeling confident and believing in ourselves. They are irrational and false, and yet they seem convincing to us because they justify our need to remain in our comfort zones.

Common limiting beliefs sound like this:

- I am not ready
- I am not as worthy as others
- I don't have enough resources
- I am incapable of doing things others have done

The world seems more complicated than it actually is when we doubt our abilities.

Leveraging Weaknesses

Despite what you think about your weaknesses or how they affect you, they may have a greater impact on your life than you realize.

Have you ever heard the expression "the best generals in war are underperformers in peacetime"?

I would like to share a personal experience with you from a time when I struggled with my mental health. Do not worry, I will keep it short and get to the point quickly.

During that time, it felt like it was the end of the world for me, and that there was no way out.

In retrospect, it forced me solve my problems with what I had and what I knew in order to cope with my thoughts and feelings. By recognizing my own internal resistance to things and learning how to let go and surrender, I started feeling better. As a result, I became more empathetic toward others, and became more creative in solving problems. I was forced to learn how to handle adversity, navigate complex challenges, and become, in my opinion, a better and more resilient person. The irony is I never thought any good would come from that phase, and never really cared or wanted anything other than to feel better. It was a biproduct, in the most paradoxical way.

Your neurotic behavior, your depression, your anxiety, or even your self-perceived dark side might all serve as pathways to superpowers you never thought you had. In times of crisis, they could provide you with the tools you need to cope, and even perform, exceptionally well.

The best way I can summarize my perspective on this subject would be to say this: If you've ever adopted the philosophy that things are not always as they seem, then consider perceiving your own weaknesses as such.

Diagnosis Precedes Remedy

When we choose to avoid business challenges today and opt to delay the inevitable, then it is only a matter of time before these challenges compound and reality bites back.

The ability to investigate and identify the root cause(s) of a problem, rather than addressing its symptoms, distinguishes a good problem solver from a mediocre one.

But identifying problems, let alone their root causes, is not always a straightforward exercise.

Most of the time, the corrective actions for these problems do not come easily or seamlessly. In most cases, they require a change of some sort. And in most cases, change is uncomfortable.

DEMYSTIFYING CHANGE

It is no secret. We are creatures of habit. We crave structure, certainty, and comfort.

When something comes along that threatens our habitual pattern of behavior, some of our initial reactions include tension, irritation, and resistance.

However, change is a constant phenomenon that never stands still. In fact, we might be better off treating it as an inevitable reality that has to be managed, rather than pretending it doesn't exist.

In today's fast-paced business environment, only organizations that can change and adapt smoothly can thrive.

Unsurprisingly, some organizations require complex engineering of change to succeed in disrupting the status quo. Employees get used to the old ways of doing things, and the leadership might not have all the answers they need to make their proposed changes seem like "a good thing".

Regardless of the organization's nature, some techniques and methods can be used to facilitate change, even in the most stagnant environments.

EFFICIENT CHANGE MANAGEMENT

The process of change management works best when we minimize transition costs, showcase results and progress, and involve all relevant stakeholders.[xxvii]

Engage Individuals and Teams and Manage Change Dynamics

It helps when leaders can offer a convincing reason to their relevant stakeholders as to why change is required. It helps even more when those leaders are good storytellers, capable of engaging their teams in the design and implementation of the change process.

Manage People Issues

As soon as we sense change is coming, our survival instincts kick in and we start to wonder whether we will be able to cope, or the extent to which we will be affected.

If people see opportunity in change, they are more likely to embrace it. And if leaders can showcase that opportunity, then they will have an easier time bringing skeptics onboard.

Support and Enable New Ways of Working

Sometimes change will require new ways of doing things. To meet expectations, leaders need to support the design and implementation of new business processes. They will also need to allocate resources for new tools, if required.

Monitor Change

Change needs to be planned, measured, and monitored. It affects different stakeholders in different ways. Leaders can calibrate their messaging and actions to the needs, requirements, and limitations specific to each stakeholder category by showing how proposed changes will affect them. That way, each stakeholder group could be more effectively served by specific actions if necessary, without derailment to the progress of other stakeholders.

LAST MILE

There you have it, folks.

Those were a few quick and easy pages to remind you of the soft skills, biases, and limitations that can influence value creation.

Without a doubt, exemplary leadership makes unlocking value in areas such as corporate governance, corporate strategy, and strategic finance easier and smoother.

You will find it easier to pick up on skepticism and resistance from within the organization and figure out how to get those that matter on your side.

You will leave a lasting impression, especially if you invest in the right people and their leadership development, who will in turn pass your legacy on.

In this way, a multiplier effect for leadership is created, enhancing collective leadership within the organization.

There is no better feeling than passing something you truly value to someone you admire and respect, with full certainty that it is in safe, reliable, and respectful hands.

It is always more advantageous to act than to dwell on ideas. Therefore, below is a proposed action framework in relation to what we have been discussing.

TAKE ACTION: Get the Ball Rolling Today

The first step on the journey to progress is creating the right climate for it.

It may be wise to gather the support of those with influence in the organization before announcing and presenting change initiatives to the rest of the affected groups.

If the key stakeholders in the organization are sold on your vision, they will help alleviate a lot of the expected resistance from those most affected by what is yet to come. They will help everyone see opportunities instead of threats, which will save meaningful time and energy for the organization.

Consider addressing the following issues in your discussions with key leaders before making any announcements to the organization at large:

- What are the problems that prompted the search for change? Were other alternatives considered?

- What are the proposed changes? Are they executable? What resources need to be allocated for such initiatives?

- What is the expected impact of the proposed changes on the organization? What do various stakeholder groups stand to gain or lose?

- How soon can the benefits be realized? Are there any major risks involved?

- What are some of the key objections that are likely to arise, and what could be done to provide assurances and mitigate negativity?

- Are incentives available to encourage change within the organization?

After preliminary discussions are complete, consider the following communication framework across the wider organization:

- Explain how the whole idea of change came about and how it has been studied and processed.

- Give people time to process the information and the effect the transition will have on them.

- Describe how the proposed changes could benefit the organization and the risks involved in implementing them.

- Give people an opportunity to participate in those changes.

- Keep communication and feedback channels open. In times of uncertainty, everyone needs assurance and clarity.

- Conduct regular meetings to monitor progress and keep everyone updated.

You could also get the momentum going and ensure accountability by putting together a working party list. This list would include people from within the company and/or external advisors. For each person, highlight their title, contact details, and their function within the organization. You can also highlight their level of involvement and responsibility, as well as the specific actions they are expected to take.

WHAT DREAMS MAY COME

The great use of life is to spend it for something
that will outlast it.

—William James, Philosopher and Psychologist

ENABLING THE ENABLERS

Well done, you! You've progressed through a range of technical and non-technical information, that admittedly isn't the sexiest, to reach this point. That takes grit and deserves recognition! We're going to bring everything together in this chapter, so don't put down the book just yet. But first, let's have a quick refresher of the overarching framework we've been using one last time.

Value Creation Enablers

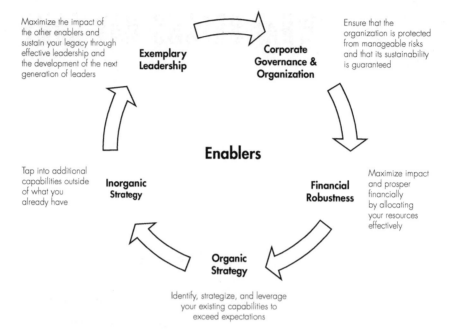

Wisdom Bites

Our discussion of each value creation enabler has focused on the main function it plays in an organization, along with the impact it could have on a firm if it were applied effectively.

We have also proposed initiatives and actions that could be addressed within each of these enablers, so that the journey towards value creation, and the benefits that can be unlocked from it, can begin as quickly and as easily as possible.

Legacy-Governance Synergy

For our first enabler, we've discussed the importance of corporate governance and the merits of developing a governance mindset. We explained that its key purpose is to protect a business and its assets, and to help put it on a path to sustainability and long-term success, even after the current leadership leaves.

Some of the key initiatives we discussed under corporate governance include:

- Having a capable Board of Directors to oversee key decisions within the organization, and act in the best interests of all its stakeholders.

- Implementing an optimal organizational structure comprised of qualified, top-tier management.

- Decentralizing decision-making by empowering competent management and having a reporting structure that respects reporting lines.

- Defining business-specific policies, procedures, processes, and systems.

- Implementing a risk management framework to actively manage and mitigate business risks.

- Ensuring that data is reliable, timely, and consistent by adopting an effective reporting framework.

Please refer to the chapter on corporate governance for more on this subject.

Numbers Game

Afterwards, we discussed how businesses can generate richer cash flows and attain a higher valuation by optimizing the allocation of assets and resources.

Some of the key ideas we discussed within strategic finance include:

- Understanding working capital and optimizing its use within business operations.

- The pros and cons of raising debt compared to equity, as well as the key features of each instrument.

- Typical valuation methodologies and what to look out for when valuing companies.

- Implementing creative financing options to free up capital and realize growth plans, including sale-and-leaseback transactions and stock market listings.

Please refer to the chapter on strategic finance for more on this subject.

Bulletproof Strategy

We then explored how to improve efficiencies and grow both organically, by leveraging existing resources, and inorganically, through mergers and acquisitions.

The initiatives discussed under organic and inorganic strategy include:

- Having the right pricing and product strategy

- Taking a strategic approach to sales and marketing

- Enhancing operational efficiency

- Improving company culture

- Leveraging data

- Recognizing the potential of intangible assets

- Identifying acquisition targets in key markets and executing inorganic initiatives

Please refer to the sections on organic and inorganic strategy for more on this subject.

Magical Charisma

Lastly, we highlighted leadership qualities and soft skills that integrate well with the other enablers. We emphasized the ability of these qualities to act as a catalyst in value creation and to increase its likelihood of success.

Some of the ideas we discussed in this chapter include:

- Empathy and conscientiousness

- Negotiation, persuasion, and storytelling

- The understanding and overcoming of irrational biases and limiting beliefs

- Succession planning

- Managing Change

Please refer to the section on exemplary leadership for more on this subject.

SHARPENING YOUR SWORD

A person who can handle everything independently is impressive, but one who is surrounded by experts who specialize in different areas makes a far greater contribution.

Yet, the reality is that asking for help is not something we are always comfortable with. Add to that the need to commit resources, or skepticism toward the value an outsider can bring to what we are trying to achieve, and it might look like the help we need isn't worth pursuing.

The fact remains, however, that everyone who is influential and successful has experts around them, from heads of state to CEOs of large companies, to famous artists.

By bringing in experts to help you on your journey, you can outsource workstreams that you don't particularly enjoy, don't have time for, or cannot excel at, so you can focus your energy on the high-impact items that you do enjoy.

It also prevents you from making costly mistakes down the road. To protect themselves against certain risks, large investors hire advisors who provide market insights, competitor benchmarking, and legal advice before they commit billions of dollars to a deal.

The most successful people aren't always the smartest, but they're the ones constantly surrounded by the brightest individuals they can find.

Acknowledging that you need expert advice in certain areas and knowing where to find it are two good "aha" moments to come across.

Instead of relying on trial and error and staying longer in a suboptimal state, why not make the most of your efforts?

The Power of Kaizen

Kaizen is a Japanese word that translates to "continuous improvement" or "little change for the better." The concept of Kaizen has been prevalent in Japan since the 1880s. Continuous improvements are a central facet of Japanese culture, and, by extension, business culture. This approach is prevalent in everything from cuisine to martial arts.[xxviii]

But what does Kaizen have to do with what we've been discussing?

Well, it is an interesting concept that might transform your odds of achieving your aims.

Imagine the following scenario: you set an ambitious strategy that you are happy with, but instead of acting in line with your usual patterns of behavior, you focus solely on one thing: taking one simple step forward. The trick here is not to jump from step 1 to 100 right away. Instead, you should focus on getting from step 1 to 2, and then build on that, one simple step at a time.

I know this might sound like a silly suggestion. Due to my lazy nature, I had skipped steps and had gotten frustrated with how long things took in the past. The more effective approach would have been to focus on one thing at a time, move forward one simple step at a time, and continue to build on each step continuously.

We can all apply a little dose of Kaizen to our goals and trust that the little steps we take will ultimately yield the intended results. Is it so bad to try something new?

MOVING FORWARD AND NEXT STEPS

By taking a methodical, calculated, and pragmatic approach to value creation, you can create a better legacy and achieve a higher valuation.

The value enablers drive the desired outcome through the compound effect of small changes. This entails breaking a business into small pieces, identifying which of those pieces will have the greatest impact when tweaked, and then taking calculated action afterward.

Nothing herculean or magical needs to be done, just a few small changes here and there will get the snowball rolling.

We will examine a hypothetical yet exhaustive case study containing all the enablers in the next few pages.

Final Case Study

Consider a hypothetical company called "Love123" that we are looking to assist with value creation.

Let's assume that Love123's valuation is derived using a multiple of net profits, which means that for Love123 to become more valuable per the valuation methodology used, we will need to figure out how to make it more profitable.

One way to increase net profits is by increasing prices while keeping the cost structure unchanged. Love123 does not have an impossible task if customers are not doing business with them solely because of pricing and/or if Love123 has a unique positioning in the market. This is especially true if these price increases are reasonable. We also know that revenue is price multiplied by volume. Therefore, if the company sells 10,000 units per year at an average price of USD 1,000 per unit, its total yearly revenue is USD 10 million.

Let's say the company makes a net profit margin of 20% on that revenue or USD 2 million per year. Let's also assume that businesses in the same sector and the same market are being acquired at a multiple of 10x (times) net profits. This means that by using precedent transactions to derive the valuation of Love123, the business is valued at USD 20 million (10 * USD 2 million).

If we increase prices by 5%, then the average price Love123 is charging per unit will increase from USD 1,000 to USD 1,050.

Again, we are claiming that the business is not affected by the price increase because of its differentiated positioning in the market and because 5% is not an increase that would lead to customers switching companies.

With this change, Love123 will continue to sell 10,000 units a year, but at an average price of USD 1,050 per unit instead of USD 1,000 per unit, which increases its yearly revenue by 5%, from USD 10 million to USD 10.5 million.

But how does this increase in revenue impact net profits?

Net profits will also increase, but the percentage increase will be larger than the percentage increase in sales, since the majority of the additional USD 0.5 million in sales will trickle down to the bottom line.

Allow me to further elaborate.

We can assume that pretax profits are USD 2.5 million before the price increase of 5%, and that a 20% tax rate applies to pretax profits.

This means that at the start of this exercise, net profits were:

- Pretax profits * (1-tax rate) = USD 2.5 million * (1-20%) = USD 2 million

Given the sale volumes remain unchanged, and the cost structure of Love123 stays the same, the additional USD 0.5 million in sales will trickle down to pretax profits.

Therefore, an additional USD 0.5 million to pretax profits implies the following:

- ADJUSTED pretax profits = USD 2.5 million + additional USD 0.5 million from the price increase = USD 3 million
- ADJUSTED net profits = ADJUSTED pretax profits * (1- tax rate) = USD 3 million * (1- 20%) = USD 2.4 million

As a result of the 5% increase in prices, the net profits would increase by 20%, from USD 2 million to USD 2.4 million.

In addition, this implies a 20% increase in valuation from USD 20 million to USD 24 million given the valuation is equal to net profits multiplied by 10x.

Thanks to the price increase, Love123 is able to increase its profits and valuation.

The above scenario is entirely hypothetical and was simplified for illustrative purposes. But you get the idea.

As we move forward, let's look at a few proposed initiatives that are expected to create more value such as:

- Ensuring the optimal organization structure is attained with all necessary functions adequately staffed.

- Increasing the autonomy of employees who have demonstrated good judgment by decentralizing decision-making.

- Having the proper controls in place to ensure that roles and responsibilities are upheld across departments and reporting lines are not crossed.

- Researching the market and identifying a need for a product or service Love123 can easily provide, using its existing capabilities and know-how, and testing that product in the market and launching it.

- Signing a mutual referral agreement with another company in a complementary field to promote cross-selling between the two companies. For each customer referred, 30% of the profits are paid to the referring company.

- Negotiating better payment terms with long-term suppliers.

- Liquidating aging inventory to free up cash stuck in unsold products and items. Discounts or liquidation sales can be beneficial when the demand for such items has slowed, releasing trapped cash back into the company so it could be reinvested into other products.

- Introducing a new client acquisition manager whose primary responsibility is to hire new clients.

- Integrating an online store to compliment the brick-and-mortar set-up. Working with an agency to establish a sales funnel through which leads can be attracted and converted into online customers.

- Establishing a "no-value created no payment" incentive scheme across the organization, which will incentivize mid- and junior-level employees to bring in business through a well-documented and reliable framework. If they elect to do so, they only receive payment for activities over and above their usual responsibilities.

- Adapting the pitch for new customer acquisition and aiming to increase conversion by 1% as a start. Small changes when compounded do make a difference.

- Performing a study into the rental yields in key areas of Love123's operations to determine whether the average rental yield in the market is lower than what Love123 is currently paying. If yes, then arranging a meeting with the landlord to discuss possible rent reductions.

- Quantifying the excess cash on the balance sheet and developing a strategy to generate a return on it, which may include investments in new equipment, new acquisitions, or financial products based on liquidity requirements.

- Merging with or acquiring a business that enhances market positioning and unlocks cost and revenue synergies.

- Identifying ways to reduce the tax burden, if applicable, with the help of an advisor.

- Being listed on the stock exchange with a valuation premium over competitors because Love123's shares would have liquidity while competitors remain private.

- Implementing a rebranding campaign and getting featured in the media in order to improve market perception and perceived value of the company's products.

- Enrolling the top leadership team in leadership training.

- Giving back to the community.

The list above is by no means exhaustive. The initiatives highlighted are highly generic as business needs vary. There could be a variety of short-term, medium-term, and long-term initiatives that could be transformational for a business, depending on the context and market conditions.

CLOSING REMARKS

Here's a universal truth that we all conveniently ignore at times: No amount of theory in the world will make any difference unless it is backed by the right actions.

The good news is that this book provides you with a template for the right actions.

Even if you strongly believe that nothing in this book can be applied to your corporate setup, you are encouraged to interpret any of the suggestions in here in the way you choose and use them to develop your own set of initiatives across your company.

The reason I recommend you go through that process is because you will be forced to consider most, if not all, aspects of value potential within the context of your own corporate setup.

Begin with small steps and small changes, then build on them one step at a time. The key is to simply begin.

I will leave you with one final consideration as we reach the conclusion of our journey. I referred to legacy more than once in this book, which might have left you wondering why.

It is no secret that we all have a desire to find a deeper meaning in what we do, especially when we are dedicating a meaningful part of our lives to doing something.

Ultimately, we want to believe that our existence made a difference and served a meaningful purpose. As we strive to leave behind something we are proud of, our lives and work take a whole new meaning.

I will leave you with a final set of questions for your consideration:

- What kind of organization do I wish to leave behind?
- What will I regret not doing on my business journey?
- What capabilities and resources do I want to leave behind?
- How do I want to be remembered by those who matter to me?
- Is there anything I can do that the world will thank me for?

I truly believe we commit a sin when we think there isn't more to our story. Don't die with the painting inside you unfinished. You know you're capable of making great things happen.

REFERENCES

[i] *What Makes Great Boards Great*. Harvard Business Review. (2021). Retrieved 30 October 2021, from https://hbr.org/2002/09/what-makes-great-boards-great.

[ii] *Board of Directors*. Corporate Finance Institute. Retrieved 30 October 2021, from https://corporatefinanceinstitute.com/resources/careers/jobs/board-of-directors/.

[iii] *Improving Performance: Flexible Organizational Structures*. Performancemagazine.org. (2019). Retrieved 30 October 2021, from https://www.performancemagazine.org/flexible-organizational-structures/.

[iv] Barnes, D. (2001). *Understanding business*. Routledge in association with the Open University.

[v] H*ow to Create a Risk Management Plan for Your Project*. Northeastern University Graduate Programs. Retrieved 30 October 2021, from https://www.northeastern.edu/graduate/blog/risk-management-plan-risk-register/.

[vi] *The holy grail of effective leadership succession planning*. Deloitte Insights. (2018). Retrieved 30 October 2021, from https://www2.deloitte.com/us/en/insights/topics/leadership/effective-leadership-succession-planning.html.

[vii] *SEC.gov | Beginners' Guide to Financial Statement*. Sec.gov. Retrieved 30 October 2021, from https://www.sec.gov/reportspubs/investor-publications/investorpubsbegfinstmtguidehtm.html.

viii *EBIT vs EBITDA*. Corporate Finance Institute. Retrieved 30 October 2021, from https://corporatefinanceinstitute.com/resources/knowledge/finance/ebit-vs-ebitda/.

ix *Six steps to releasing 'trapped' cash from your business*. Bmim-cash-flow.co.uk. (2019). Retrieved 30 October 2021, from https://www.bmim-cash-flow.co.uk/post/how-to-fix-working-capital.

x Di Muzio, T., & Robbins H, R. (2016). *Debt as Power*.

xi *Valuation Methods*. Corporate Finance Institute. Retrieved 30 October 2021, from https://corporatefinanceinstitute.com/resources/knowledge/valuation/valuation-methods/.

xii *Pros and Cons: Going Public - FindLaw*. Findlaw. Retrieved 30 October 2021, from https://www.findlaw.com/smallbusiness/business-finances/pros-and-cons-going-public.html.

xiii HENGSBERGER, A. T*rend research: how to identify relevant trends*. Lead-innovation.com. Retrieved 30 October 2021, from https://www.lead-innovation.com/english-blog/trend-research.

xiv *Budgeting and business planning*. Infoentrepreneurs.org. Retrieved 30 October 2021, from https://www.infoentrepreneurs.org/en/guides/budgeting-and-business-planning/.

xv Landis, T., Balinas, T., & Myers, E. (2021). *Customer Retention Marketing vs. Customer Acquisition Marketing | OutboundEngine*. OutboundEngine. Retrieved 30 October 2021, from https://www.outboundengine.com/blog/customer-retention-marketing-vs-customer-acquisition-marketing/.

xvi *How to Create an Efficient Product Strategy*. Shopify. (2020). Retrieved 30 October 2021, from https://www.shopify.com/partners/blog/product-strategy.

xvii *How to Determine the Right Pricing Strategy for Your Business*. https://www.uschamber.com/co. Retrieved 30 October 2021, from https://www.uschamber.com/co/run/finance/pricing-strategies-for-your-business.

xviii *Citibank Guide: Basic Business Operations*. Citigroup.com. Retrieved 30 October 2021, from https://www.citigroup.com/citi/citizen/community/data/guide6_eng.pdf.

xix   *Culture Kings: 27 Company Culture Examples to Get You Inspired.* Built In. Retrieved 30 October 2021, from https://builtin.com/ company-culture/company-culture-examples.

xx   *Intangible Assets.* Corporate Finance Institute. Retrieved 30 October 2021, from https://corporatefinanceinstitute.com/ resources/knowledge/accounting/intangible-assets/.

xxi   *Top tips for scaling a business* Retrieved 30 October 2021, from https://www.tonyrobbins.com/business/scaling-a-business/.

xxii   *Strategic Alliances: Power Your Inorganic Growth Strategy.* Deloitte United States. Retrieved 30 October 2021, from https://www2. deloitte.com/us/en/pages/mergers-and-acquisitions/articles/ strategic-alliances.html.

xxiii   *Due Diligence in 10 Easy Steps.* Investopedia. Retrieved 31 October 2021, from https://www.investopedia.com/articles/ stocks/08/due-diligence.asp.

xxiv   *An Introduction to Technical Due Diligence.* Implementconsultinggroup.com. Retrieved 31 October 2021, from https://implementconsultinggroup.com/media/6854/ technical-due-diligence.pdf.

xxv   *What Are the Characteristics of a Good Leader?* | CCL. CCL. Retrieved 31 October 2021, from https://www.ccl.org/articles/ leading-effectively-articles/characteristics-good-leader/.

xxvi   *Cognitive Biases: The Ultimate List of Human Irrational Decisions. HumanHow.* Retrieved 31 October 2021, from http://humanhow. com/list-of-cognitive-biases-with-examples/.

xxvii   *The Hard Side of Change Management.* Harvard Business Review. Retrieved 31 October 2021, from https://hbr.org/2005/10/ the-hard-side-of-change-management.

xxviii   Inside Kaizen: Continuous Improvement. Investopedia. Retrieved 31 October 2021, from https://www.investopedia. com/terms/k/kaizen.asp.

ABOUT THE AUTHOR

Karl Yaacoub has over 11 years of experience in investment banking and private equity. He began his career at Standard Chartered Bank, a British multinational financial institution listed on the London and Hong Kong Stock Exchanges, where he completed assignments and deals in Asia, Europe, and the Middle East.

He then joined a newly formed investment company with a capital of USD 680 million that had just been listed on the Dubai Financial Market (DFM), where he was responsible for sourcing and assessing investments in the Gulf Cooperation Council (GCC), Europe, and Asia.

As a dealmaker, Karl has worked on deals in many different industries, including oil and gas, chemicals, technology, healthcare, and education.

He has worked closely with a wide range of professionals from top investment banks, private equity firms, sovereign wealth funds, management consulting firms, family offices, and legal firms. His network of international colleagues, investors, and friends is among his greatest assets.

Karl is Chartered Financial Analyst (CFA®) and holds a Bachelor of Engineering (BE) in Electrical and Computer Engineering.

Karl is a Chicago Bulls fan. He enjoys live music and great meals with great company. He can be reached by e-mail at karl@tgovc.com.

Lightning Source UK Ltd.
Milton Keynes UK
UKHW040705160223
417122UK00001B/150